BARBAROSSA
THROUGH SOVIET EYES

BARBAROSSA
THROUGH SOVIET EYES

The First Twenty-Four Hours

Artem Drabkin and Alexei Isaev

English text
Christopher Summerville

Pen & Sword
MILITARY

First published in Great Britain in 2012 by
Pen & Sword Military
an imprint of
Pen & Sword Books Ltd
47 Church Street
Barnsley
South Yorkshire
S70 2AS

ISBN 978 1 84415 923 9

Pen & Sword Books Ltd incorporates the imprints of
Pen & Sword Aviation, Pen & Sword Maritime,
Pen & Sword Military, Pen & Sword Family History,
Wharncliffe Local History, Wharncliffe True Crime,
Wharncliffe Transport, Pen & Sword Discovery, Pen & Sword Select,
Pen & Sword Military Classics, Leo Cooper, Remember When,
The Praetorian Press, Seaforth Publishing and Frontline Publishing

Printed in U.S.A.

Contents

Author's Note

In 1942 my father, Vladimir Drabkin, should have graduated from the Moscow Energy Institute. That did not happen. In June the previous year he volunteered for the Red Army, along with thousands of other men and women, following the German invasion of the USSR, code-named *Barbarossa*. In the autumn of 1941 my father – now a platoon commander in the 133rd Infantry Division – was seriously wounded. A period of hospitalization and further training in an officer's school followed. He finished the war with the rank of lieutenant, serving as a meteorologist in the 45th Long-range Bomber Aviation Division.

Many years later, my father and his friends would sit round the table and – after a few shots of vodka – recount tales from the war, some funny, some sad. I would sit in the corner unnoticed, quiet as a mouse, so as not to get sent to bed: for the stories of veterans were not for children's ears . . .

Time passed and I matured with a sense of duty to the generation that raised me: what could I do to preserve the receding era? I decided to record the memories and experiences of the wartime generation and share them with others. That is how the *I Remember* website (www.iremember.ru) was born. The website is now ten years old and, along with my associates, I have collected more than a thousand interviews with veterans. And as long as this remarkable generation survives, we will continue our work.

Many of the sources in this book are drawn from the interviews mentioned above; others are drawn from Soviet and German archive material or published monographs. For the reader's convenience quotes have been numbered: the corresponding source may be found in the 'Sources' section at the back of the book.

Artem Drabkin
Moscow, 2011

Timeline:

21–22 June 1941

N.B. Moscow time is one hour ahead of Berlin time.

21 June 1941
12.00: Gerhard Kegel, a Soviet agent in Moscow's German embassy, informs his superiors that 'war will break out within the next forty-eight hours'.
13.00–17.00: German Panzer units ordered up to their start line on the Soviet border.
19.00–20.15: Meeting in Stalin's Kremlin office. First news of impending war received.
20.00–21.00: Three German servicemen defect and are detained on the Soviet border. They confirm that war will begin on 22 June.
20.50–22.20: Stalin decides to put troops in the near-border districts on battle alert.
23.00: German and Finnish naval vessels begin mine-laying operations in the Gulf of Finland.
23.50: Admiral Nikolai Kouznetsov, Chief of the Soviet Navy, directs his units to 'switch to Operational Readiness No. 1 with immediate effect'.

22 June 1941
00.30: Directive No. 1, signed by Timoshenko and Zhukov, is issued to Red Army units, warning of possible German attack.
01.00–02.30: Unsuccessful attempt by German special forces (Brandenburg Regiment) to penetrate the Soviet border near Augustów.
01.15: Black Sea Fleet put on Operational Readiness No. 1.
02.15: General Pavlov, Commander of the Western Special Military District, orders commanders of the 3rd, 4th and 10th Armies to deploy troops according to their secret pre-war instructions – the so-called 'red packets'.
03.45: Soviet cargo ship *Gaisma* is sunk en route from Riga to Lübeck.
03.50–05.00: German aviation strikes Soviet aerodromes and rail junctions.

04.05: Germans open up a 30-minute artillery barrage along the Soviet border.

05.00–05.30: In Berlin, the Soviet Ambassador, Vladimir Dekanozov, is officially informed of the outbreak of war. In Moscow, the German Ambassador, Schulenburg, hands over Hitler's 'declaration of war' to Viacheslav Molotov, the People's Commissar of Foreign Affairs.

06.30: Admiral Kouznetsov authorizes the Soviet Navy to initiate mine-laying operations.

06.40–07.00: Soviet bombers from the 7th Aviation Division raid Tilsit.

0700: Stalin issues Directive No. 2 to the Red Army, instructing units to repel the invaders where found.

07.15: German bombers strike airbases at Kiev, capital of the Ukraine.

08.00: German motorized units from the 7th Panzer Division reach Kalvaria.

08.30–09.00: German mechanized units go into action, threatening Taurage, Siauliai, Kibartaj, Kaunas, Kalvaria and Alytus.

09.00: German troops from the 291st Division occupy Palanga.

09.35: Kouznetsov, Commander of the Northwestern Front, reports: 'Enemy tank and motorized units are breaking through towards Druskeniki.'

11.00: German troops occupy Brest, although Soviet fighters hold out in the Citadel and train station.

12.00: Viacheslav Molotov informs Soviet citizens of the outbreak of war via radio. Italy declares war on the USSR.

12.00–13.00: Units from the 18th Panzer Division clash with the Soviet 30th Tank Division in the first tank versus tank action of the Great Patriotic War.

13.00: German troops capture Taurage.

14.00: Units from the 3rd Panzer Group capture two key bridges across the River Neman near Alytus.

14.00–16.00: Stalin announces 23 June as the 'first day of mobilization'.

21.00: Stalin issues Directive No. 3 to the Red Army, calling for an immediate counter-offensive.

24.00: Advance units from the German LVII Panzer Corps (3rd Panzer Group) reach Varenai (Lithuania, Kaunas Region), having pushed 70km in a single day.

Preface

On land, in the skies, at sea
Our song is mighty and stern:
If war comes tomorrow
Or the march we've got to join,
Be ready for it today!

('If War Comes Tomorrow' – popular Soviet song)

At 3 a.m. on 22 June 1941, a telephone rang in Berlin's Soviet embassy. An unfamiliar voice declared that Reichsminister Joachim von Ribbentrop was awaiting Soviet representatives at the Ministry of Foreign Affairs in Wilhelmstrasse. German translator, Paul-Otto Schmidt, later recalled that:

> I never saw Ribbentrop as agitated as he was five minutes before the arrival of Vladimir Dekanozov, the Soviet Ambassador. He was nervously pacing back and forth like a beast in a cage: 'The Führer is surely right . . .' he said, as if to calm himself, '. . . The Russians will attack *us* if we don't act now.' He scurried from corner to corner, repeating these words. Vladimir Dekanozov was led into the office at the appointed time. Unaware of the situation, he stretched out his hand to Ribbentrop before sitting and, on the instructions of his Government, began asking questions that demanded concrete explanations. But the stone-faced Ribbentrop interrupted: 'It is of no consequence. The hostile posture of the Soviet Government towards Germany, and the serious threat posed by troop concentrations on the German border, have forced the Reich to undertake countermeasures . . .'[1]

Valentin Berezhkov, the Soviet interpreter, recorded in his memoirs:

Ignoring the fact that, for several weeks, the Soviet embassy, on instructions from Moscow, had been trying to draw attention to flagrant German violations of the State Border, Ribbentrop declared that Soviet troops had invaded German territory, although this bore no resemblance to reality.[2]

The Soviet delegation was obliged to sit through a reading of Hitler's twelve-page memorandum, which, instead of a formal declaration of war, announced the Führer's intention to 'repulse [Soviet] aggression by all the means at [Germany's] disposal'. Ribbentrop would add nothing further and the meeting broke up without the usual handshakes.

Meanwhile, in Moscow, the German Ambassador, Count Schulenburg, had requested a meeting with Viacheslav Molotov, the Soviet Minister of Foreign Affairs. With 'deepest regrets', Schulenburg handed over Hitler's memorandum. According to Schulenburg's aide, Gustav Hilger,

Viacheslav Molotov looked tired. After the Ambassador made his announcement, silence fell. Molotov was obviously trying to suppress his agitation. Then, raising his voice, he said that the Ambassador's words were nothing short of a declaration of war – indeed, German troops had already crossed the border and aircraft were bombing Odessa, Kiev and Minsk. Then he gave vent to his indignation. Having declared that Germany had invaded a country with which it had a non-aggression pact, Viacheslav Molotov ended with the following words: 'We have not deserved it . . .'[3]

Maps

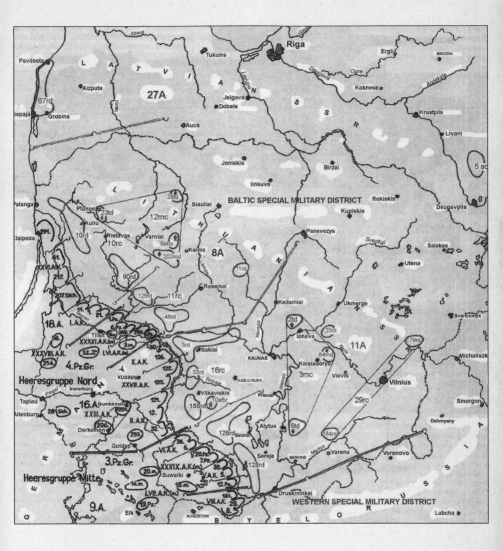

Map 1

The Baltics: German and Soviet force deployment on 21 June 1941 in the northern sector of the front.

Legend

A – army	mc – mechanized corps	rd – rifle division
A.K. – army corps	md – motorized division	sich – security division
ac – airborne corps	pz – panzer division	SS – SS division
atbr – anti-tank brigade	Pz. Gr. – panzer group	td – tank division
m – motorized division	rc – rifle corps	

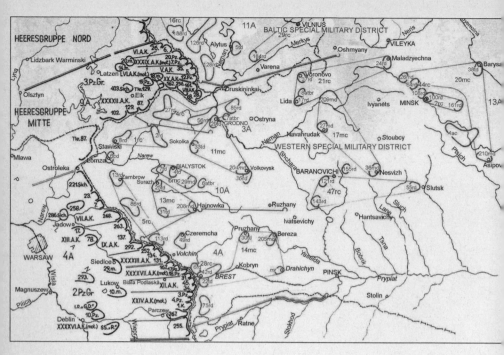

Map 2

Belorussia: German and Soviet force deployment on 21 June 1941 in the central sector of the front.

Legend

A – army	mc – mechanized corps	rd – rifle division
A.K. – army corps	md – motorized division	sich – security division
ac – airborne corps	pz – panzer division	SS – SS division
atbr – anti-tank brigade	Pz. Gr. – panzer group	td – tank division
m – motorized division	rc – rifle corps	

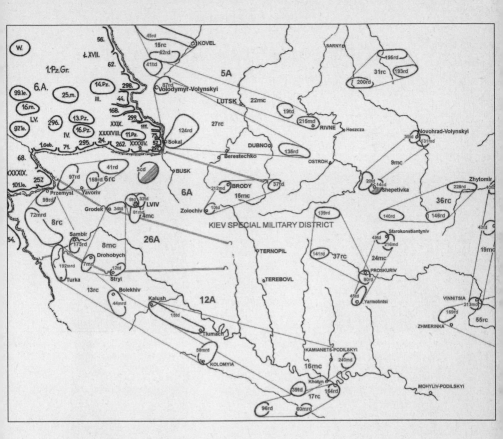

Map 3
Ukraine: German and Soviet force deployment on 21 June 1941 in the southern sector of the front.

Legend
A – army
ac – airborne corps
m – motorized division
mc – mechanized corps

md – motorized division
pz – panzer division
Pz. Gr. – panzer group
rc – rifle corps

rd – rifle division
td – tank division

Photo Album:
Supremos, Soldiers and Survivors

Supremos

Josef Stalin, Supreme Commander.

Viacheslav Molotov, Narkom of Foreign Affairs.

Semen Timoshenko, Narkom of Defence.

Georgi Zhukov, Chief of General Staff.

Nikolai Vatoutin, First Deputy Chief of General Staff.

Nikolai Kouznetsov, Narkom of Soviet Navy.

Fedor Kouznetsov, Commander of the Baltic Special Military District.

Dmitri Pavlov, Commander of the Western Military District.

Mikhail Kirponos, Commander of the Kiev Special Military District.

Maxim Pourkaev, Chief of Staff of the Kiev Special Military District.

Grigory Shtern, Commander of the Far East Front.

Ivan Kopets, Commander of the Western Special Military District Air Force.

Filipp Oktyabr'sky, Commander of the Black Sea Fleet.

Soldiers

Alexander Korobkov,
Commander of the
4th Army.

Leonid Sandalov,
Chief of Staff of the
4th Army.

Vasili Kouznetsov,
Commander of the
3rd Army.

Mikhail Potapov,
Commander of
the 5th Army.

Ivan Mouzychenko,
Commander of the
6th Army.

Petr Sobennikov,
Commander of the
8th Army.

Pavel Ponedelin,
Commander of the
12th Army.

Alexei Kourkin,
Commander of the
3rd Mechanized
Corps.

Pavel Rotmistrov,
Chief of Staff of the
3rd Mechanized
Corps.

Dmitri Ryabyshev,
Commander of the
8th Mechanized
Corps.

Pavel Belov,
Commander of
the 2nd Cavalry
Corps.

Nikolai Dedaev,
Commander of the
67th Rifle Division.

Ivan Roussyanov,
Commander of the
100th Rifle Division.

Mikhail Sakhno,
Commander of the
56th Rifle Division.

Efim Pushkin,
Commander of the
8th Tank Division.

Timofei Mishanin,
Commander of the
12th Tank Division.

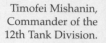

Semen Bogdanov,
Commander of
the 30th Tank
Division.

Mikhail Katoukov,
Commander of the 20th Tank
Division.

Survivors

Pavel Ankundinov.

Mikhail Badanes.

Lazar Belkin.

Vladimir Boukhenko.

Alexander Bourtsev.

Semen Danich.

Ion Degen.

Petr Delyatitsky.

Nikolai Doupak.

Ivan Garshtya.

Ivan Gaidaenko.

Sergei Gorelov.

Olga Khod'ko.

Vitaly Klimenko.

Alexei Maximenko.

Mariana Milyutina.

Nikolai Obryn'ba.

Vsevolod Olimpiev.

Vladimir Osaulenko.

Nikolai Ovsyannikov.

Alexander Panuev.

Yuli Routman.

Mikhail Sandler.

Grigory Sinyavsky.

Rostislav Zhidkov.

Daniil Zlatkin.

Petr Grishenko.

Chapter 1

'If War Comes Tomorrow'

Hitler's objectives for the war against the USSR were formulated on 31 July 1940 at a Berghoff conference:

> We will not attack England but we will break those illusions that fuel England's will to resist, then anticipate a change in her position. England's hope lies with Russia and America. If belief in Russia is wrecked, America will fall away from England, as the destruction of Russia will entail an incredible strengthening of Japan in East Asia.[1]

German leaders thus sought a way out of strategic deadlock via the invasion of Russia, since they were unable to resolve the fate of the war by landing in the British Isles. At the same time, the defeat of Russia – the last potential enemy on the Continent – would allow the Germans to redirect their industry towards the production of naval and aviation assets in preparation for a showdown with the British.

Development of Hitler's plan of campaign against the USSR began in August–September 1940. In December the same year it took shape as Directive No. 21, better known as the *Barbarossa* plan. The objective of the operation was as follows:

> The main Soviet land forces, located in Western Russia, should be destroyed by bold operations via the deep and rapid advance of Panzer pincers. Any retreat by the enemy's battleworthy troops into the vast expanses of Russian territory ought to be prevented.[2]

After the annihilation of the main Red Army units, the territory west of the Archangel–Astrakhan Line would be occupied. The mobilization capability of the USSR – in other words, its ability to raise new military formations – was assessed as insufficient for recuperation after such a blow. German troops allocated for *Barbarossa* were divided into three Army Groups: North, Centre and South. The armies of Germany's allies – Romania, Hungary and Finland – were also to be engaged in the operation.

Russian leaders correctly assessed Germany as a major potential enemy – as did most Soviet citizens – but Stalin's successful anti-Fascist propaganda campaign (depicting Nazism as Public Enemy No. 1 following Hitler's rise to power) and the rough treatment meted out to German Communists was toned down in 1939. After the Molotov-Ribbentrop Pact of that year, the bogeyman of Fascism began to recede in the minds of ordinary Russians. Hitler was still seen as a menace, but faith in the infallibility of their leaders seemed to guarantee security for the Russians; and so the following phrases were common:

> 'There will not be a war once we've concluded the non-aggression pact with the Germans.'

> 'We trade with Germany and send wheat, oil and coal for them. Why should they want war?'

> 'Molotov didn't visit Hitler for nothing. They agreed on peace.'

In fact, on the Russian side, there was genuine anxiety regarding provoking German aggression, as war veteran Vladimir Boukhenko remembers:

> after the signing of the 'non-aggression pact' with Germany, everything possible was done to observe it, so that no minor excuse might be exploited by the Germans as a pretext for war. I remember just such an occasion. While at college, I'd been given a place at a summer leisure camp. All kinds of amateur performances were organized there. I knew a poem about the heroic struggle of the German people [connected with the abortive Marxist uprising of January 1919 – ed.] and decided to recite it at one of the concerts. But the camp officials wanted to hear the poem first, just in case it contained anything that might offend the Germans. Just think, even in

student summer camps they thought about such issues, so concerned were they not to provide Hitler with an excuse for war![3]

These sentiments were augmented by the perception of Germany as a heterogeneous society, in which a part of the population – proletariat and peasantry – supposedly cherished kindly feelings towards their fellow workers in the Soviet Union. Herbert Wehner, a German Communist exiled to Russia in 1935, wrote:

> During the peak of the German-Russian pact, anyone with eyes to see noticed signs of madness among many Communist propagandists. A Russian functionary, Samoilovich, who'd had a chance to visit the Polish provinces [i.e. the eastern portion of Poland, following the German–Soviet invasion of that country in 1939 – ed.], told me that German troops looked with envy at the red stars of the Soviet soldiers, and a whole regiment had, upon the request of the Germans, presented their badges and buttons as mementoes and signs of goodwill. Episodes such as these, which were hard to verify, led to the conclusion that German–Soviet 'friendship' would lead to a softening of the situation inside Germany, and that pro-Russian sentiments among the German population would become an obstacle to Hitler's military ambitions.[4]

A veteran of the Great Patriotic War, Lev Maidanik, remembered:

> One day, we sat in a forest meadow during political education classes. A discussion was held about the non-aggression pact with Germany and I asked a question: 'Comrade *Starshy Politruk* [Senior Political Officer – trans.], why do trains crammed with our wheat, timber, ore and other goods constantly roll to Germany?' The Senior Political Officer looked at me, smiled for some reason and asked, quite off the point as it seemed to me, 'How old are you?' – 'Gonna turn twenty soon, Comrade Starshy Politruk.' – 'OK, you're only twenty and you don't understand that a German proletarian who eats Russian bread will never raise his hand against Russia. That is what proletarian solidarity is about. Thus, a

German worker will not fight a Russian worker. That's why the trains with bread and other stuff roll to Germany. Is that clear?' – 'Clear, Comrade Starshy Politruk,' I mumbled.[5]

In general, it may be said that before the war there had been no distinct image of the foe in the minds of Russian men born between 1919 and 1922 (and it was they who would absorb the initial shock of *Barbarossa*). In this regard the soldiers and officers of the Red Army were inferior to those of the Wehrmacht, guided by simple and clear statements, such as the following from General Hoepner: 'the purpose of the struggle is the ruination of Russia, so it must be conducted with unprecedented brutality [. . .] First of all, no mercy to the representatives of the current Russian Bolshevist system . . .'. At this point, it is appropriate to quote the words of war veteran, Nikolai Obryn'ba: 'We were unprepared for the war not so much technically as morally, and it would take time to re-educate people. It was one of the factors that gave the Germans an opportunity to overwhelm our Army.'[6] Thus it was necessary to teach people to hate: in other words, to fire up their determination to fight. This meant demonizing the Germans to make it clear they represented a mortal danger, not only on a personal level for soldiers in combat but on the grand scale: here was a real threat to the nation, to the Motherland. But in June 1941, the lack of a clear and potent image of the foe was coupled with a blind overconfidence in the might of the Red Army, which, according to the popular song, 'If War Comes Tomorrow', was supposed to smash the enemy 'with little loss of blood and a powerful blow'. This overconfidence was the result of effective Soviet propaganda (which boosted Red Army successes in local conflicts), augmented by the recognition that, by the end of the 1930s, the military profession was one of the most prestigious and highly paid in the country. Mikhail Sandler, a sergeant in the automobile company of the 65th Tank Brigade, stationed near Lwów, recalls:

> All soldiers were well clothed and shod. We were fed better than we would have been in civilian life. We ate gruel with meat every day, except for the so-called 'fish day'. Soldiers were rationed with *makhorka* [coarsely milled tobacco – trans.]

and paid wages [7 roubles a month – trans.]. With this money we bought tooth powder, undercollars [i.e. a strip of disposable white material sewn into a military blouse to keep it clean – ed.], but couldn't afford cigarettes, as a pack cost 35 *kopecks*. I don't remember if we were allowed to get money transfers from home. A deputy platoon commander received 36 roubles a month, a *starshina* [sergeant major – trans.] on extended service had a monthly package of nearly 500 roubles plus food ration. Many of the guys were eager to stay in the forces for extended service.[7]

And after all, the rationing system had been abolished in the country only at the end of the 1930s. It was practically impossible to buy clothes. It wasn't by accident that owners of a 'Singer' sewing machine could always rely on a reasonable income – people brought clothes for 'turning': that is, turning old clothes into new. In the cities people lived in communal flats, sometimes seven people in a room 10m^2.

Another veteran, Rostislav Zhidkov, living in the city of Tula, remembers:

I was an ordinary guy of that time. I was fond of mechanics and kept myself busy in hobby groups – aircraft modelling, radio. Back then it was like this: you study badly, they won't accept you; or if you got a grade '2' [the lowest – trans.] – go away until you improve!

We played soccer, 'street versus street'. The ball was made from a bladder. Each of us was responsible for the ball on a weekly basis: one had to keep it fixed – it was a crucial duty! We had to stitch the skin of the bladder, and if you tightened it too much you'd have your face smashed by the other guys. There was no gear. There was food – we ate alright. A bike, a pocket watch and a socket-powered radio-set – they were luxuries and objects of envy in those days. In Tula, a push-bike was number one.

Adult men attended the circus to watch wrestling. The circus in Tula had been built in the days of Ivan Poddubnyi [a famous Russian wrestler in pre-Revolutionary times – trans.].

Workmen would give us boys tickets for the first two parts [of a performance], and we watched shows of actors and animals, and before the third part, when the wrestling was supposed to happen, we would go outside and give the tickets back.

Then we were accepted into the sports society 'Pishevik' [literally, 'food industry worker' – trans.] to play in a kids' soccer team. They kitted us up – team strip, gaiters, and boots. We were to play at a stadium. Then I found myself in a junior team. I did well on the right wing. We passed grades such as: Be Ready for Labour and Defence, Be Ready for Sanitary Defence, Young Voroshilov's [surname of the Soviet People's Commissar of Defence in those days – trans.] Shot – it was well developed.[8]

Life in the countryside was even harsher, although some men, including Dmitri Boulgakov, who lived in the Kursk *Oblast* [administrative region – trans.] back then, reckoned that by the eve of war things had improved a good deal:

There was a good harvest in 1937 – we were given 3 kilos of bread for a day's work! In 1938 the harvest was weaker but still reasonable. In 1939 they began to deliver more goods to the shops. What was the most delicious thing for me then? White bread! A cake or bun, sugar, candies – any sweets – all that was a luxury for us.

We waited until someone went to the city and brought us a present. Did I have a watch, a push-bike, a portable gramophone, a radio-set? In 1941 my brother came home for vacation and brought a gramophone. It was something special! Half the village would come around to listen to it. In the countryside a gramophone was a marvel. Teachers, the postmaster, and the school principal's children had bikes. They wouldn't allow us to have a ride. Some people had striking-clocks. Only people who did intellectual work – the medical attendant, the school principal – had watches. One teacher had a pocket-watch.[9]

The Army could not only clothe, shoe and feed up boys who hadn't yet fully recovered from the famine of early 1930s, but could also give them a new profession. War veteran, Alexander Bourtsev, remembers:

> Each of us dreamed of Army service. I remember that guys were coming home like different people after three years of service. A village simpleton had left but a literate, cultured man – physically a much stronger one – well-dressed in Army blouse, breeches, and jackboots had returned. He was capable of working with machinery, of being a leader. When a *slouzhivyi* [ex-serviceman – trans.], as they were called, returned from the Army, the whole village would gather. A family was proud of the fact that he'd served in the forces, that he'd become such a man. That was what the Army gave.[10]

Among Soviet servicemen, however, the airmen and tankers stood out. Unlike other combat arms, which wore khaki uniforms, airmen wore blue and tankers steel-grey, so their appearance on the streets did not go unnoticed. They were also remarkable on account of their decorations – a great rarity back then – and for this reason they were highly honoured. They were glorified in movies such as *Hot Days*, *If War Comes Tomorrow*, *The Fighter Pilots*, *The Fifth Squadron* and others. Thus the romantic image of tankers and airmen was shaped by the superstars of Soviet cinema.

In those days the arts – especially cinema – were hugely influential. The fact the Army was largely manned by semi-literate youngsters – blindly faithful to the established social system and its leaders (even among the Officer Corps only 7 per cent had tertiary military education, and more than one-third hadn't fully completed secondary schooling) – permitted the authorities to manipulate soldiers' perceptions with ease. But patriotic films and songs celebrating the invincibility of the Red Army caused complacency, creating a false impression of the coming war as a mere parade. That said, the psychological climate in the Armed Forces was quite different from what we are accustomed to now, having inherited from the Revolutionary times ideas of equality between officers and privates. Vladimir Sinaisky, a veteran fighter regiment mechanic, recalls:

> it helped us that there was no barrier between officers and soldiers. Although there were commanders and recruits, we

were all Red Army fighters. Once, when a woman addressed us with a request to show her something and called us 'soldiers', one of our comrades said: '*Mamasha* [mummy – trans.], we are not soldiers, we are Red Army fighters. Our dads and granddads used to thrash soldiers and officers during the Civil War.'

Relations between commanders and privates were, I would say, almost friendly. There was a Red Army House in the garrison, and having stepped over its threshold, you became a member of the community. There were sports halls, dance halls, a cinema, a restaurant. And having come to the Red Army House, we rank-and-file could dance with the commanders' wives or have a snack in the buffet. A similar order existed in the medical unit. If someone fell ill a doctor would say: 'Forget that you are commanders and privates, in here you are all sick servicemen. You're all equal to me.'[11]

But a lot changed when, at the end of 1930s, the USSR began increasing Army numbers in preparation for the 'big war'. The armies of those Military Districts along Russia's western border were reinforced by youths from the recently incorporated republics – Western Ukraine (formerly part of Poland – ed.), Belorussia, the Baltic States – and of course, their loyalty was more than dubious. Mikhail Sandler remembers:

In 1940 many 'Westerners' joined the Army, and there was an inflow of recruits from Central Asia (prior to that, as a rule, the men from Central Asia had served in the National Territorial Divisions). Many of them had problems with the Russian language or the fundamentals of handling technical equipment. There was no mockery of them – everything was explained patiently.[12]

Meanwhile, Stalin's wave of repressions and purges – although not as significant as customarily depicted (*see* Fig. 1 on page 9) – had led to considerable changes in the ranks of the Officer Corps. At the senior and medium levels, which had suffered most, gaps were filled by promoting junior commanders who lacked the necessary experience and skills. Most junior commanders had been raised via the pre-term graduation of military cadets (by order of the People's Commissar of Defence, Marshal Semen Timoshenko, on 14 May 1941). Perhaps the most significant aspect of the purges was the atmosphere of dread and insecurity left in their wake. Taking into account the almost fivefold increase of troop numbers compared to 1934, as well as lack of training and inexperienced leadership, the Red Army of 1941 could hardly be considered 'regular'.

Fig. 1: Table showing loss of Soviet line and political officers from Officer Corps (excluding Air Force and Navy), 1934–1939, based on: RGVA, f. 37837, op. 18, d.890, pp. 4–7; RGVA, f. 37837. op. 19, d.87, pp. 42–52. Quoted by N.S. Cherushev, 'Statistika armeiskogo terrora' ('Statisitcs of Army Terror'), Military History Archive, 1998, No. 3, pp. 41–49.

REASON	1934	1935	1936	1937	1938	1939
Non-political*	1,513	6,719	1,942	1,139	2,671	197
Illness/death	4,604	1,492	1,937	1,941	941	1,150
Criminal**	479	349	728	4,474	5,032	67
Political***			257	11,104	7,718	277
TOTAL	6,596	8,560	4,918	18,658	16,362	1,691
REINSTATED (1938–1940)	–	–	–	4,661	6,333	184
REVISED TOTAL (%)	5.8%	7.2%	3.9%	9.7%	5.6%	0.5%

* Non-political – alcoholism, incompetence, voluntary resignations etc.
** Criminal – those arrested and sentenced.
*** Political – those deemed 'enemies of the people' and expelled from the Communist Party.

And on top of all this, a bitter blow was dealt to the prestige of the military elite – the airmen – by Timoshenko's Order No. 0362, which stated that all graduates of military schools must begin their service as sergeants instead of lieutenants. Furthermore, airmen with less than four years' service were obliged to live in barracks. Salaries and allowances were changed accordingly – in other words, downgraded. The final insult for these men came when they were stripped of their right to wear the officer's eagle insignia [known colloquially as the 'chicken' – trans.]. Many pilots took offence and refused to wear rank badges as a sign of protest. Meanwhile, it frequently happened that lieutenant technicians had to report an aircraft's condition to their commander, who was a sergeant, thus violating the basic military principle of subordination. Veteran flyer, Ivan Gaidaenko, remembers:

> In December the notorious order of the *Narkom** [People's Commissar – trans.] of Defence Timoshenko had been issued. I – a lieutenant, a flight commander, an order-bearer – was placed into barracks! And to make matters worse, as a flight commander, I was also appointed barrack senior. Just imagine, lieutenant-pilots have arrived from schools – the flying personnel – and they immediately get demoted to sergeant. And what is more, they are not just confined to barracks, but they also get stripped of their rank insignia! What a disgrace in front of our girls, acquaintances, kinfolk! Of course, discipline collapsed after this, making it difficult for me to control this gang of young flyers. We certainly did what we were supposed to do according to the flight training program, but the flyers drank heavily and would go AWOL. And if they didn't have enough money for booze, the guys would sell their bedlinen (the barrack was fitted out with brand-new blankets, pillows, bed-sheets). One *Komsomol* [i.e. Communist Union of Youth – ed.] member had 'distinguished' himself in this way. He was called up to a meeting and questioned: 'Why do you

---

*Eager to avoid 'bourgeois' terminology such as 'Ministry of Defence' or 'War Office', the USSR's military was overseen by the People's Commissariat of Defence, known as the 'NKO' (*Narodnyi kommissariat oborony*) or 'Narkomat' in Soviet jargon. It was fronted by a designated commissar – the 'Narkom' – and in June 1941 Marshal Timoshenko (a personal friend of Stalin) occupied that post. Meanwhile, the Red Army had a General Staff, known as the 'GshKA' (*General'nyi shtab Krasnoi Armii*). Once war broke out, however, the structure and nomenclature of the USSR's military command underwent a series of changes. On 30 June 1941 Stalin inaugurated the State Defence Committee or 'GKO' (*Gosudarstvennyi Komitet Oborony*) – a kind of 'War Cabinet' with himself as Chairman and Viacheslav Molotov as his deputy. The GKO exercized authority over all Government departments, both civilian and military. On 8 August 1941 Stalin created the SVGK or 'Stavka' (*Stavka Verkhnogo Glavnokomandovaniia*) to function as a purely military High Command with himself as Supreme Commander. The Stavka and the Red Army General Staff were both answerable to the GKO.

drink, disgrace yourself? We'll expel you from the *Komsomol*!'
And his reply was: 'Big deal! Do it! I'll be a non-Party
Bolshevik!' I guess the outbreak of the war saved me –
otherwise they would have sent me to jail for the loss of State
property . . .'[13]

Such were the fighting men born between and 1919–1922, who had
become the backbone of the Red Army by 22 June 1941: ill-assorted,
with controversial perceptions and double standards, disorientated
with regard to the character of the oncoming war and the real nature
of the enemy. The nation's leaders appreciated the situation better
than ordinary citizens, but even they couldn't fully comprehend the
prospects of approaching events. As for the Red Army soldiers
themselves, the voice of one *Barbarossa* survivor speaks for many:

> Even before we left for summer military camp we heard
> rumours of impending war. Many commanders sent their
> wives to stay with relatives deep in the interior. We frequently
> heard of provocations from the German side – breaching of
> the border, shooting incidents and so on. But despite this,
> Army commanders and political officers tried to convince us
> that everything was under control. Nevertheless, our fears and
> forebodings did not leave us. And what was worse, our
> Sergeant Frolov – who, at the best of times, could never stop
> singing – began crooning sad songs round the clock. Still, it
> didn't stop him from daydreaming: he constantly talked of
> how he would return home to his parents and beloved girl;
> how they would get married and really start to live. We
> listened with envy . . .[14]

Soviet leaders expected the main German strike to be dealt from
the west, across Belorussia towards Moscow – the heart of the State.
Defensive plans were drawn up accordingly, allowing for the
absorption of initial enemy strikes and an immediate counter-
offensive from Ukraine into German-occupied southern Poland. By
destroying enemy units in this area, Soviet leaders hoped to stall any
advance into Belorussia. Officially referred to as 'Considerations for
Strategical Redeployment', the scheme became known as the
'Primary Operation Plan'.

Soviet districts that bordered German-controlled territory were designated 'special'. In total there were three such districts: 'Baltic', 'Western' and 'Kiev'. Prior to the launch of *Barbarossa*, the Special Military Districts contained garrison troops as well units assigned to border protection – the so-called 'covering' armies. In case of war, the three districts were to form operational Army groups or 'Fronts', bolstered by Red Army reserves arriving from the interior. 'Covering' armies consisted of regular troops tasked with holding the USSR's western border during the initial mobilization and deployment of the Red Army. Fully manned – even in peacetime – 'covering' forces usually included mechanized and air assets, and could be deployed within hours. That said, their role was never intended to be more than a stop-gap until full mobilization of the Red Army. During questioning undertaken by the Military Scientific Department of the General HQ in the 1950s, the former head of the operations section of the Kiev Special Military District, Ivan Bagramyan, declared that:

> The troops directly engaged in cover operations [. . .] had minutely developed plans and documentation down to the level of a regiment inclusive; all other troops of the District [. . .] had a special sealed envelope containing operational orders and instructions regarding the implementation of pre-arranged tasks kept in the safe of each unit's chief of staff. Plans of action and detailed documentation had been developed in the District HQ only for corps and divisions. The executive officers could access these only after unsealing the aforementioned envelopes.[15]

But it should be mentioned that, in some cases, plans had not been conveyed to executive officers. General Petr Sobennikov, Commander of the 8th Army of the Baltic Special Military District (a border-protection or 'covering' force) writes in his memoirs that:

> On 28 May 1941, I (together with the Chief of Staff, Major-General Georgi Larionov and a Member of the Military Counsel, Division Commissar Sergei Shabalov) was summoned to the District HQ, where the Commander, Colonel-General Fedor Kouznetsov, hurriedly acquainted us

with the defence plan [for the District]. All this was conducted in a hasty manner, the situation being somewhat tense [. . .] All the notes I had made [during the meeting – trans.] were taken from me and we were ordered to depart for the duty station, having been promised that the defence plan instructions and our working notebooks would be sent to Army HQ immediately. Unfortunately, we didn't receive any instructions, let alone our working notebooks.[16]

Meanwhile, awareness of the coming storm was running through the USSR. A resident of Moldavia, Ivan Garshtya, remembers:

We were simple peasants, didn't read newspapers, and had no radio. For example, I remember how great an event was the first movie demonstration in our village. It was *Peter the Great*, and since there was no screen it was projected onto the wall of a white house: so, after that, people were coming up and touching this wall in wonderment [. . .] We knew and understood little, but that year I remember adults storing up salt, matchsticks, kerosene [in preparation for the hardships of war – ed.]. Just before the war, almost all Jews from our village had managed to leave. Only the four poorest families remained.[17]

And Mikhail Badanes, a military cadet of Stalin's Military Academy of Mechanization and Motorization RKKA, recalled that in May 1941 he and his fellow students were lined up on the parade ground before being sent on a month-long probationary period: 'The head of our group addressed us: "Take all necessary belongings and equipment required for war. Most likely you'll be sent to the front straight from probationary period."'[18] Another cadet, Rostislav Zhidkov of the Tula Armour-Technical School, also remembered those days:

First there was the war in Ethiopia, then the Finnish one [i.e. the Italian invasion of 1936 and the Soviet invasion of 1939, respectively – ed.]. Thus the sensation of an approaching crisis had been growing. Voroshilov's 'spurt' marches were introduced – 25km on skis will full kit (20 kilos). That was brutal. After the first march four guys found themselves in hospital. From January 1941 our training program began to change. They took away mathematical analysis and English, but increased the number of practical exercises. From January 1941 we began to patrol the railroad and instead of six hours of lectures, now we had nine or ten. We slept while sitting. At the end of May, twelve men from our drill company were commissioned, having been made lieutenants ahead of schedule.[19]

Meanwhile, Petr Delyatitsky, a soldier stationed in the Ukrainian town of Lutsk, remembered that, in spring 1941, the local population began taunting the Red Army garrison: 'Soon the Germans will kick your arses outta here!' Delyatitsky added that 'The air around us seemed to be filled with hatred.'[20]

The growing danger was felt especially acutely in those districts located on the USSR's western border. Pavel Ankundinov, a future ground-attack pilot, recalled that,

Rumours of the coming war were circulating constantly. In April I went for vacation to see my first cousin, Vladimir Melnikov, in Polotsk, where he was head of the political department in an army division. He met me with these words: 'What have you come for? The war is gonna break out soon. Leave this place.'[21]

In summer 1941 Ankundinov's cousin found himself trapped in a pocket, encircled by Germans. Later he commanded a partisan outfit called 'Melnikov's Brigade'.

According to Vladimir Vinogradov, a soldier stationed in the Ukrainian town of Rovno, situated some 200km from the border, he and his comrades were roused by daily alarms the week before war broke out:

At 5 or 6 a.m. we would head off in vehicles for a quick raid in the direction of the border and then return to barracks, have breakfast, and begin routine field drilling. Some units of the 5th Army, in which I served, were located right up against the border. Information about the situation on the opposite bank of the frontier river [the Bug – ed.], was alarming: there were reports that German troops were mustering, that there was continuous movement and that optical devices were being used to observe our territory. There were border violations by German aircraft. All this created an atmosphere of tension. At night-time, military units marched through Rovno, aircraft flew towards the border over the town. As it turned out later, they were based at frontier aerodromes or large forest glades. Of course, all this indicated that the situation was complicated, that military action might break out in the near future. Several days before 22 June a TASS [Telegraph Agency of the Soviet Union – trans.] announcement was released. It contained a refutation of the rumours regarding a German attack, but we took this as confirmation of the fact that war was approaching – and fast. I visited a photography shop, got my picture taken, and sent home my last photos of peacetime . . .[22]

Nevertheless, some Soviet citizens remained blissfully oblivious as the country teetered on the abyss. Olga Khod'ko remembered that,

Having graduated from a teacher's college in 1937, I began work in a Zaborodskaya primary school [a village in the Leningradsky region – ed.], and within three months I was transferred to Ustie, where I taught Russian language and literature in a *semiletka* [a seven-year school – traditionally, schools were called by their duration of study – trans.] for another year before the outbreak of the war. Neither I nor my kinfolk had a sense of approaching war. On the contrary, it seemed that the harsh 1930s were over and now our life would begin to go right . . .[23]

Back at the western border, however, the situation was tense and the Headquarters Staff of the Military Districts increasingly fretful. Consequently, district commanders frequently raised issues with their superiors in Moscow. Matvei Zakharov, Chief of Staff of the Odessa Military District, remembered:

On 6 June, the Military Counsel of the Odessa District asked the Chief of the General HQ to allow him to redeploy the 48th Rifle Corps to the most likely location of enemy action. When permission was granted, the 74th and 30th Divisions, plus the Corps Staff, took up new positions a little to the east of Beltsy. This was achieved by 15 June.[24]

But not all decisions made by the commanders of near-border districts were supported from above. Sometimes local leaders were pulled up sharply. For example, a telegram of 10 June 1941, sent by the Chief of the General Staff to the Commander of the Kiev Special Military District (KOVO), stated:

> clarify for the People's Commissar of Defence for what reason
> units of the fortified sectors of the KOVO have been ordered
> to deploy at advanced positions. Such actions may immediately
> provoke the Germans to engage in combat with unforeseen
> consequences. Immediately cancel this order and report who
> exactly made such an arbitrary directive. [Signed] Zhukov.[25]

On 11 June commanders of the Military Districts were instructed not to deploy field units or those from fortified sectors at advanced positions. On 12 June the Narkom of Defence ordered: 'All Air Force flights in the 10km-wide near-border strip to be banned.' The latter measure was most likely undertaken to prevent an accidental border violation due to navigational errors. The prohibitive measures were closely accompanied by actions aimed at reinforcing the Special Districts. On 12 June the Kiev Military District Command was informed of the scheduled arrival of the 16th Army from the Trans-Baikalian Military District. The arrival of the troop trains was planned to take place between 17 June and 10 July. The following units were expected to arrive:

- Army control structures with the service units
- 5th Mech[anized] Corps (13th, 17th Tank Divisions and 109th Motorized Division)
- 57th Tank Division
- 32nd Rifle Corps (46th,152th Rifle Divisions,126th Corps Artillery Regiment.[26]

In reality, the mustering of the 16th Army began on 18 June – an example of the forwarding of troops prior to the commencement of hostilities, a common procedure during the final days of peace.

On 14 June, the Chief of Staff of the Kiev Military District, General-Lieutenant Maxim Pourkaev, demanded a round-the-clock operational watch in all HQs based in the Kiev Military District. On the same day, in the light of the growing threat of invasion, the Odessa Military District received instructions to detach the 9th Army's HQ and station it at Tiraspol (i.e. closer to the border and the area of troop concentration – ed.). But the most significant event of 14 June was the following TASS announcement in *Izvestia* (a newspaper, the title of which translates as 'The Latest News' – trans.):

Even before the arrival in London of the English [*sic*] Ambassador to the USSR, Mr Cripps, and especially afterwards, rumours of the 'approaching war between the USSR and Germany' began to be exaggerated in the English and foreign media. According to these rumours, Germany had purportedly presented the USSR with a set of territorial and economic claims [. . .] It has been stated that the USSR rejected these claims and has begun preparations for war with Germany, mustering troops near the border with the latter country. Despite the obvious silliness of these rumours, responsible circles in Moscow considered it necessary [. . .] to authorize TASS to announce that these rumours are a piece of deceitful propaganda, run by forces hostile to the USSR and Germany, whose interests lie in future expansion via the unleashing of war. TASS announces that Germany has not presented any claims to the USSR [. . .] and in light of this, no negotiation on the subject has occurred. According to information available to the USSR, Germany has been strictly observing the conditions of the Soviet-German Non-Aggression Pact [. . .] and in view of this, in the opinion of Soviet circles, rumours concerning German intentions to breach the Pact and undertake an attack on the USSR are groundless; and the current transfer of German troops [. . .] towards the eastern and north-eastern territories of Germany has no connection with Soviet-German relations. The USSR, as is readily apparent from its peaceful policy, has observed – and intends to observe – the conditions of the Soviet-German

Non-Aggression Pact, and in view of this, rumours that the USSR is preparing for war against Germany are false and provocative. The current training of Red Army units and proposed [military] manoeuvres are aimed at nothing more than the drilling of reservists and the checking of the railroad network, which, as is well known, are conducted on an annual basis. To portray these activities as hostile to Germany is, at the very least, inappropriate.[27]

Most ordinary Russians saw in the TASS announcement only the words: 'rumours concerning German intentions to breach the Pact and undertake an attack on the USSR are groundless'. But the bulletin was not meant for domestic consumption. Anatoly Khonyak, a veteran, remembers:

Just before the war I was sent to the Belorussian Military District. Our unit was located at Kobrin, but in June we departed for a summer training camp near Kolki. Of course there was an atmosphere of tension, especially after the TASS announcement of 14 June, which cast doubt on press releases concerning the deployment of German troops on our borders. Of course it was done to prevent provocations.[28]

It was nothing less than an invitation for the German leadership to conclude a negotiated settlement on vexed questions or turn the conflict into an open stand-off via sabre-rattling. But the deathly silence that ensued served as a signal for the Soviets to begin mobilization.

Chapter 2

Sons of the Homeland

During the last week of peace, preparations were conducted at a rapid pace. All leave for military personnel was cancelled in the middle of June, as reserve units began moving up to the border. General Sergei Iovlev, commander of the 64th Rifle Division (44th Rifle Corps), remembered that

> On 15 June, Army General Dmitri Pavlov, commander of the Western Special Military District, ordered the divisions of our corps to prepare for redeployment with full complements. The directive called for embarkation on 18 June. We were not informed of our destination – only the signals units knew it. The embarkation was conducted in the camps and at Smolensk, and this extraordinary situation made people wary; one could read an uneasy question in their eyes: is it really war?[1]

The forwarding of troops from the interior to the line of the Dvina and the Dnieper rivers in the west became a priority task in the middle of June 1941. Nikolai Biryukov, commander of the 186th Rifle Division, recalled that

> On 13 June we received a directive of special importance, according to which the Division was supposed to move to a 'new camp'. The location of the new camp was not known – even to me, the Division Commander. Only after we passed Moscow did I discover that we were to muster in the forests west of Idritsa: that is, on the line of old fortifications along the former Soviet–Latvian border, which existed before 1939.[2]

But the decision to transfer troops from the interior districts up to the border had been made hopelessly late: these units would not influence events on the first day of the war. At the end of May, according to Alexander Panuev, who served in a howitzer regiment of the 17th Tank Division (16th Army):

> My battery won first place in a divisional contest for marching and firing-drill, so they granted me a holiday. I'd caroused for a couple of weeks when I got a cable: 'Return to your unit immediately.' When I made my reappearance, the 16th Army was being transferred to the West. We embarked during the first days of June and rolled along the Trans-Siberian main line. Our tank division and regiment was supposed to go to Vinnitsa, but then the TASS article denying the movement of troops was published and we were diverted to the *Tursib* line [Turkestan-Siberian railroad connecting Siberia and Central Asia – trans.]. All open trucks were packed with plywood stuff, in order to give the impression that machinery was being transported for the sowing campaign. The train would stop only where water was available, but when we passed through large stations even the hatches were closed. The heat that June![3]

The wave of Red Army movements engulfed the 'covering armies' soon after the TASS announcement. On the night of 16/17 June, units of the 62nd Rifle Division (5th Army) quit the Kivertsy camp in the Kiev Special Military District. Having completed two night marches they arrived at new positions near the border by the morning of 18 June. Nevertheless, no defence line was taken up, and the division dispersed to local settlements and forests. From 17 June, the Commander of the 41st Rifle Division, Georgi Mikoushev, began mustering divisional units in a summer camp. On 18 June, the Commander of the 5th Army ordered the withdrawal of the 45th Rifle Division from the training ground. On the same day, 18 June, the 135th Rifle Division, comprising the second echelon [i.e. second line or reserve – ed.] of the 27th Rifle Corps (5th Army), was ordered up to the border. It was to move to the Kivertsy camp, recently vacated by the 62nd Division. The commander of this division, General-Major Fedor Smekhotvorov, remembered after the war:

> On 18 June 1941 the 135th Rifle Division marched off from the area of permanent deployment (Ostrog, Dubno,

Kremenets), and by the end of 22 June arrived at Kivertsy (10–12km north-east of Lutsk) . . .[4]

But the most radical measures were undertaken by the Baltic Special Military District. On 18 June, District Commander Fedor Kouznetsov's Order No. 00229 – 'on the setting up of combat readiness' – was issued, putting the anti-aircraft defences and signals system of the District on full combat alert. As well as conventional procedures, Kouznetsov ordered the establishment of mobile detachments for landmine anti-tank operations in the direction of Telsiai, Siauliai, Kaunas and Kalvaria. These detachments – manned by soldiers from pioneer units – were to be supplied by motor transport, allocated by the Motorcar-Armour departments. Kouznetsov ordered the detachments to be ready by 21 June and also ordered mechanized and rifle units closer to the border. A soldier of the 2nd Battery/358th Artillery Regiment (126th Rifle Division), Sergei Matsapoura, remembers:

> On the 18th, all units of the Combined Detachment were roused by alarm again. There was to be a quick march along the coast, followed by embarkation on a train. When we arrived at Siauliai, we understood that we were on our way to the border. Suddenly the guys became more serious, mentally preparing for what lay ahead. We rode from Siauliai to Kaunas with frequent stopovers – sometimes up to half a day long. On the night of 22 June we arrived at our destination. We took post near some Lithuanian town. The battery commander explained that the border was about 30km away. Right of us and a bit ahead, beyond a pine grove, the 501st Battery of the Howitzer Artillery Regiment was deployed. Riflemen and pioneers from our detachment took up good defensive positions. We didn't know where the main forces of the 126th Division were . . .[5]

Details concerning the deployment of Red Army and Wehrmacht troops at different sectors of the front will be given as events unfold. But for now it is worth stating that, by 21 June, Germany had managed to deploy against the USSR 77 per cent of its infantry divisions, 90 per cent of its tank divisions, 94 per cent of its motorized divisions and 100 per cent of its Air Force units.

Meanwhile, the Soviet Union had only managed to deploy 43 per cent of its divisions in the first echelon. Some 25 per cent were in the second echelon of the Special Military Districts (which were to be transformed into Fronts on the outbreak of war) and another 32 per cent were under the authority of the Supreme Command (being on the way to the border or still stationed in the interior Districts). Thus, the invasion force had a significant numerical superiority in manpower over those Red Army units that could engage them on the first day of war (*see* Figs 2 and 3 below and on page 23). Having an approximate twofold numerical superiority near the border, the three German army groups had acquired a threefold to fivefold superiority in the area of the main strikes. Most Red Army units were still scattered across the expansive territory between the western border and the Dnieper–West Dvina line.

Fig. 2: Table comparing opposing forces (divisions) on the first day of *Barbarossa*, including second echelon and reserves.

ECHELON	UNIT	SOVIET	GERMAN
First	rd (fd)	66	117
	td	24	17
	md	12	15.5
	cd	6	3.5
	Tanks	9,530	3,496
	Aircraft	7,133	4,914
Second	rd (fd)	37	13
	td	16	–
	md	8	–
	cd	1	–
	Tanks	2,848	–
Reserve	rd (fd)	Up to 77	–
	td		21
	md		2
	cd		1

Key: rd – rifle division; fd – field division; td – tank division; md – mechanized division; cd – cavalry division.

In the first hours of *Barbarossa*, only forty Soviet divisions from the 108 available in the 'covering armies' were in a position to oppose

Fig. 3: Table comparing opposing forces on the various 'fronts' or 'strategic directions'.

ECHELON	UNIT	NORTH-WEST		WEST		SOUTH-WEST	
		Soviet (PribOVO)	German (AG North)	Soviet (ZapOVO)	German (AG Centre)	Soviet (KOVO+OVO)	German (AG South+allies)
First	rd (fd)	15	21	12	27	26	47
	td	4	7	8	5	10	5
	md	2	6.5	4	3.5	5	5.5
	cd	–	–	2	1	4	2
	Tanks	1,618	1,389	2,900	810	6,089	949
	Aircraft	1,211	1,070	1,789	1,468	2,863	1,473
Second	rd (fd)	4	6	12	3	19	4
	td	–	–	4	–	10	–
	md	–	–	2	–	5	–
	cd	–	–	–	–	1	–
	Tanks	–	–	157	–	1,783	–

Key: rd – rifle division; fd – field division; td – tank division; md – mechanized division; cd – cavalry division.

the assault. The remainder were either in barracks or en route for the front. Although it is commonly understood that the Germans underestimated the strength of the USSR, this is only true of its latent assets or *potential*. In reality, the situation at the border, on 22 June, overwhelmingly favoured the attackers. General Halder – in a diary entry for 11 August 1941 – acknowledged that Soviet strength had been underestimated, but also noted that Red Army divisions: '[are] not as well armed, and not as well staffed as ours, and their tactical abilities are much weaker than ours, but still, they exist . . .'. In effect, the Germans forestalled Soviet deployment and, on the evening of 21 June 1941, massed on the border ready to strike. As dusk fell, Wehrmacht company commanders relayed a message from the Führer by lamplight:

Soldiers of the Eastern Front! My soldiers! Burdened by the load of tremendous concern, forced to keep our plans in secret for many a month, at long last I can tell you openly the whole truth. Up to 160 Russian Divisions are lined up against our border. Over many weeks borders have been constantly breached – not only the borders of Germany herself, but others as well – in the Far North and in Romania. Soldiers of the Eastern Front, at this moment our forces are so great that nothing has equalled them in the whole history of the world. Shoulder to shoulder with the Finnish Divisions and heroes of Narvik, our comrades are awaiting combat with the foe in the Arctic [. . .] You are at the Eastern Front. In Romania, on the banks of the Prut, on the Danube, along the Black Sea coast, German and Romanian forces, led by the head of state, Antonescu, stand in one formation. The greatest armies in history are ready for combat – not only because they are forced to it by severe military necessity or because this or that state needs protection, but because European civilization and culture need salvation. Soldiers of Germany! Soon, very soon you will engage in combat – in a harsh and resolute fight. The fate of Europe, the future of the German Reich, the very existence of the German nation are in your hands now.[6]

While German soldiers finalized their preparations for invasion, most Soviet citizens – unaware that, within hours, life would be divided into 'before' and 'after' – were quietly enjoying a normal Saturday night. No Russian born before 1930 could answer 'I don't remember' to the question: 'What did you do on Saturday, 21 June 1941?' The void into which the nation fell the following day was too vast, too deep, to forget. According to the words of war veteran, Nikolai Afanasiev:

Every single day between June 1941 and May 1945 everyone dreamed of the life they had left behind. And of course the last days, hours, minutes of that life – joyful, happy, peaceful – we turned over in our minds, and they seemed to be especially marvellous.[7]

It is worth citing some reminiscences of that Saturday evening, to better understand what the words 'peaceful life' meant to ordinary Soviet citizens. Daniil Zlatkin, a Muscovite, remembers:

I was on a business trip – we were building a secret installation in Theodosia Bay. I lived at the 'Astoria' hotel. I left it at 10 p.m. and, as fate decreed, got acquainted with a very attractive girl at a café. What a marvellous girl she was! A Romanian girl on vacation. I grew fond of her, invited her for a walk in the park, and bought twenty roses for her! We were sitting in a shady alley, talking about life and other stuff – she was interested in Moscow, and, since I knew nothing about Romania, I was very curious about life there. All of a sudden some man leaped out from the scrub, grabbed me by the sleeve and yelled: 'Ah-a-a-a, that's where you are! We've caught you, you bastard! I've been looking for you a long time, but at last I got you! Now, you come with me!' he was dragging me and shouting, 'Police!' Then he pulled out a whistle and began to blow. People, policemen, came from nowhere [. . .] He says: 'This is the man who steals our roses!' Everyone began to fuss and yell: 'Take him to a police station! Give him a good punch! Thrash him!' – I said: 'What? Which roses? Let me explain, I bought them!' – 'Where?' – 'I paid a cashier for them.' – 'Call the cashier!' – The cashier comes up and says: 'I don't remember this man.' – 'How come you don't know me? I bought the roses from you! Twenty of them – you had no more . . .' At that moment some man came up and said: 'Have a look and see if these roses were deflowered or cut.' A policeman glanced at this man, touched the flower stems and said that the roses had been cut. They searched me, found no knife on me, and all understood that I'd bought them. Then the cashier said: 'Oh, yes, yes, I remember now – he bought them from me indeed.' The public lost interest in me, but some man ran up and said: 'I am from the *Komsomol'skaya Pravda* newspaper, I want to write a satirical article entitled, "The Thorny Roses", where can I find you?' I said: 'I live at the "Astoria" hotel, such-and-such number.' – 'I'll come around tomorrow.' I woke at 10 a.m. but no one had come . . .[8]

Semen Danich, a platoon commander in the 565th Pioneer Battalion (294th Rifle Division), remembers:

The division camped in a forest near Lipetsk. The officers lived in tents, the soldiers in shelters made from branches. Sixteen guys had been commandeered to this division from our [military] school and we lived in harmony in the same tent.

Some of our guys got an idea to celebrate graduation from the school. Everyone liked the idea, and the most experienced and senior among us – Lieutenant Dereshev – was entrusted to organize a picnic. We agreed to have it on a beautiful island amid the Voronezh river, downstream from the Lipetsk Metal Works. We stocked up on snacks and champagne and, with the help of a girl we knew, invited her whole class of graduates. The feast began on the evening of 21 June and lasted till the morning of the 22nd. Champagne flowed like water – by the way, I tasted it for the first time in my life back then. It seemed that the whole city was rejoicing, such was the noise and cheerful laughter. In all my long life since that day, I never witnessed such a jolly celebration, beautifully illuminated as it was by bonfires . . .[9]

A student of the Dnepropetrovsk Medical Institute, Ibragim Drouyan, remembers:

We dispersed late. I saw my mates off, and when I returned, Vasya and Zhenya were already sleeping. A book, partially read, lay on the floor near the head of the Vasya's bed. Zhenya was sleeping, having rolled up. I swung open the window. Down below, the city glittered with thousands of lights, the muffled buzz of traffic bursting into the room with the cool night air. Below us, on the second floor, a gramophone was playing and girls were singing. Lime trees had broken into bloom that day and now, at night, their smell was especially fresh and pleasant.

I stepped away from the window and turned on the radio. The speaker on the wall stood silent for several seconds, then the enchanting sounds of a Strauss waltz poured from it. Marvellous, peaceful music [. . .] What a pleasure it was to listen to Strauss that night! But then, restless Zhenya began to stir and muttered something angrily with a sleepy voice. I switched off the radio, turned off the lights and lay down. But sleep would not come. I was preoccupied with preparations for the following day's celebration: I would have to iron my shirt, buy a new tie [. . .] And I would also have to send a cable to my kinfolk: 'I'll come to see you all soon!' I fell asleep thinking about that cable . . .[10]

Alexander Kopanev, a student of the Naval Medicine Academy, remembers:

> On Saturday afternoon, 21 June 1941, leaves of absence were to be granted to cadets, but they were cancelled for unknown reasons. In the evening, after dinner, the cadets were marched in formation to listen to a lecture on the international situation. The lecture was delivered by a regimental commissar from the Political Department of LVO [Leningrad Military District – trans.]. I remember his words: 'I don't know whether the war will break out tomorrow or in two weeks, but there should be no doubt that the war against Nazi Germany is inevitable . . .'[11]

At the port of Sevastopol – main base of the Soviet Black Sea Fleet – the destroyer *Soobrazitel'nyi* was commanded by Sergei Vorkov, who recalled that:

> The day of 21 June was serene. There were shoals of clouds in the blue sky. Thin acacia leaves were shrivelling up in the heat. Sevastopol was following the routine of a large coastal city that day. But the calm was superficial. Activities relating to increased combat readiness were concealed behind it. It seemed to me that the day had slipped by unnoticed and evening had arrived in an instant. I rushed to my ship. The night promised to be quiet, although the sunset was somewhat unusual. The big round loaf of the sun was slowly sinking into the sea, staining it dark purple and bathing the superstructure, masts and deck of the ship in a soft glow. I was looking at the sea, the sinking sun, and for some reason became alarmed [. . .] The ship's lights were reflecting in the small Korabel'naya Bay, located almost in front of the Minnaya mooring. A bit to the left, at the Pavlovksy Cape, a small green light flashed and blinked. I heard the midnight clock strike [and] walked up the quay. No one around. My steps resounded loudly in the night. A sea-wind was strengthening, rustling the leaves and sending clouds scudding across the sky [. . .] Refreshed by the night coolness, I returned to the ship and opened a book at my cabin desk. But I didn't feel like reading and went to bed.[12]

Ivan Roussyanov, commander of the 100th Rifle Division, remembers:

Saturday, 21 June, was a bothersome one. But the cares were pleasant. We were getting ready for the ceremonial opening of a stadium we had just built. In the evening we had a final look at the new stadium, accompanied by commanders and political officers. Everyone was very pleased, the mood festive and elated. 'Well, comrades,' I said, 'tomorrow we will have a joyful but stressful day. I command you all to get a good night's sleep, that you might be in good form – no worse than the Znamensky Brothers [famous Soviet athletes of that time – trans.]. Good night!' After exchanging a few jokes, everyone went home.

I reached the house about midnight. My family – wife, son and two daughters – were already entangled in their third dream. I prepared my uniform for the morrow's festivity, examined and cleaned my favourite *Nagan* (after being wounded in the left hand I could shoot only from a revolver) and went out to the porch. The HQ building loomed nearby, the dim outline of the stadium could be seen a bit further away. Occasionally, light gusts of wind tousled the treetops. It was completely quiet.

Our 100th Rifle Division, decorated with the Order of Lenin, was stationed in the Minsk area, in a small place called Uruch'e. The location was very picturesque. Woodland was all around – a typical, dense Belorussian forest: fir trees, aspens, and then, suddenly, a silver birch grove, shining against a dark backdrop of firs. In spring, the smell of birch juice and the bursting buds would make you tipsy, sonorous concerts of nightingales would deafen you. In summer, there were wild berries aplenty. In autumn, mushrooms [. . .] I went to bed but couldn't sleep. Anxious thoughts stole over me: when will the signals battalion return from the manoeuvres conducted by General Dmitri Pavlov's Special Military District Army? And how had my men performed there? I fell asleep imperceptibly, dwelling on these concerns.[13]

Valentina Vorob'eva, a citizen of Leningrad, remembers:

On Saturday, 21 June, our family was planning a picnic for the following day. We were to go to a park on the right bank of the Neva – one of our favourite places. Suddenly, around five o' clock in the morning, someone knocked at the door of our flat. Father opened it and a messenger handed him a summons from the military commissariat. He was astonished. It never occurred to us that the war could have started. We gathered in the corridor and father told us: 'I suppose it's a mistake of some sort. You must finish preparing for the picnic, I'll be back soon.' He never returned.[14]

Army General, Dmitri Pavlov, spent the night of 21 June preoccupied with purely peaceful things. While German soldiers listened to Hitler's address, the Western Special Military District Commander was enjoying a much pleasanter performance. Instead of bombastic banalities he was happily absorbing Molière's *Tartuffe* – the Moscow Arts Theatre touring Minsk just then. The foremost personalities of the republic had come to see this performance by the Moscow celebrities. Apart from Dmitri Pavlov, Panteleimon Ponomarenko, First Secretary of the Central Committee of the Communist Party of Belorussia, was also present at the show. The play lasted almost till midnight, whereupon Dmitri Pavlov was summoned to District HQ to be informed of events occurring on the other side of the border. As it turned out, a German deserter with Communist sympathies had crossed the frontier to tell of the coming invasion. This was confirmed in a report filed by Mikhail Bychkovsky, Commander of the 90th Border Guard Detachment of the NKVD*:

---

* The *Narodnyi Kommissariat Vnutrennykh Del* or 'NKVD' was the Soviet political police and counter-intelligence branch. Under the leadership of Lavrenti Beria, its functions were various: the control of the regular police force, the running of labour camps, intelligence operations within the USSR and abroad, plus political surveillance of military units. The NKVD also provided guards for the protection of the State Border. Each sector of the border had a frontier post on the border proper, a command post 3 or 4km inside Soviet territory and, 5 or 6km beyond that, a regimental barracks. In 1939 NKVD border troops were organized into the GUPV ('Chief Directorate of Border Troops') and fielded infantry, cavalry, reconnaissance and air units. These soldiers bore the brunt of *Barbarossa* and sustained severe casualties as a result.

On 21 June at 21.00 hours a soldier who had deserted from the German Army was arrested in the sector of the Sokal'sky commandant's office. As there was no interpreter in the office, I ordered the sector commandant, Captain Ivan Bershadsky, to transport the soldier to the Town of Vladimir and Detachment HQ. At 00.30 on 22 June the soldier arrived at the Town of Vladimir-Volynsky. At about 1 a.m. the soldier, Liskow, stated via an interpreter that the Germans would be crossing the border at dawn on 22 June. I immediately reported this to Brigade Commissar Yakov Maslovsky, the orderly on duty [at] HQ. I also telephoned General Mikhail Potapov, Commander of the 5th Army, who received my information with suspicion [. . .] I, too, was unconvinced by Liskow, but nevertheless summoned the commandants of the border sectors, ordering them to strengthen the State Border and set up special listening posts along the River Bug [. . .] At the same time I ordered them to report to me the moment anything suspicious occurred on the opposite side. I was at HQ all this time.

At 1 a.m. the sector's commandant reported that all was quiet. Since our interpreters were not so skilled, I summoned a teacher of German language from the town, and Liskow repeated the same story again – that the Germans were preparing to invade at dawn on 22 June. He called himself a Communist and declared that he had arrived on his own initiative in order to give a warning. Before I could finish the interrogation I heard heavy artillery fire coming from the direction of Ustilug. I realized the Germans were shelling our territory; the questioned soldier immediately confirmed this. I tried telephoning the commandant but communications were down.[15]

Corporal Liskow was not an immature youngster. He was 30 years old, a cabinetmaker by trade, who had worked at a furniture factory in Kohlberg (Bavaria). He had left his wife, children, father and mother to become a pioneer in the 75th Infantry Division, having been drafted into the Army in 1939. That evening his company commander, Lieutenant Schultz, announced that their unit would cross the Bug under cover of darkness in rafts, boats, and on pontoons, following an artillery bombardment. Without hesitation, Liskow swam across the Bug. Although Mikhail Bychkovsky expressed doubts regarding Liskow's information, the news reached Stalin in person as fast as lightning. Georgi Zhukov, Chief of the General Staff, remembered:

> On the evening of 21 June the Chief of Staff of the Kiev Military District, Lieutenant-General Maxim Pourkaev, rang me up and reported that a turncoat had come to the border guards – a German Sergeant Major [*sic*] – asserting that German troops were taking up the start line for the advance, which would begin on the morning of 22 June. I reported to the Narkom and Josef Stalin what had been told to me by Maxim Pourkaev. Josef Stalin replied: 'Be at the Kremlin in forty-five minutes with the Narkom.' [. . .] I rode to the Kremlin with the Narkom and General-Lieutenant Nikolai Vatoutin. On the way we agreed that we would secure a decision for making the troops ready for combat at any cost.[16]

Thus Stalin became acquainted with the general contents of Hitler's address via a German corporal.

But no immediate decision was made at the meeting. Initially, Stalin expressed doubts regarding the validity of the deserter's report. The Narkom of Defence, Semen Timoshenko, expressed the opinion – supported by all those present in military uniform – that the deserter was telling the truth. They suggested sending a directive to the Military Districts to make the troops ready for combat. Nevertheless, Stalin considered this premature. There was still some hope for a peaceful settlement of the crisis, so it was decided to instruct local commanders to clarify the situation. In other words, Soviet leaders did not exclude the possibility that, by provocative acts, German troops were attempting to goad local Red Army commanders into air strikes or cross-border raids, thereby providing Hitler with a *casus belli* (cause for war). In this case, large-scale hostilities would commence not on 22 June but on the 25th or 26th, after an intense Nazi propaganda campaign had denounced the 'Red Barbarians'. As we now know, Hitler was not considering such an option. But on the night of 21 June this was not quite so obvious.

The directive was completed in accordance with these proposals. Finally, a document, known to history as Directive No. 1, was sent to the troops:

Attention: Military Counsels of the LVO [Leningrad Military District], PribOVO [Baltic Special Military District], ZapOVO [Western Special Military District], KOVO [Kiev Military District], OdOVO [Odessa Special Military District].

Copy: Narkom of the Navy.

1. Over the period of 22–23 June 1941 [a] German attack on the fronts of the LVO, PribOVO, ZapOVO, KOVO, OdOVO is likely. The attack may begin with provocative activities.

2. The task of our troops [is] not to fall for any provocative activities likely to entail major complications. At the same time the troops of the Leningrad, Baltic, Western, Kiev and Odessa Military Districts ought to be ready for action, in order to repulse a possible sudden attack by the Germans or their allies.

3. I order:

a) on the night of 22 June 1941, secretly take up fire emplacements of the fortified sectors at the State Border;

b) by dawn of 22 June 1941, disperse the whole Air Force [i.e. air assets of specified districts – ed.] over the field airstrips [i.e. a network of airstrips designed for dispersal of air assets – ed.], including the Army co-operational aircraft [i.e. air assets subordinated to Army control – ed.], and camouflage thoroughly;

c) all troops to be ready for action. The troops to be dispersed and camouflaged;

d) anti-aircraft defence to be ready for action with no raising of reserve personnel. Prepare all measures regarding the blackout of cities and [military] objectives;

e) no other activities to be undertaken without a special directive.

Timoshenko, Zhukov.

21 June 1941[17]

Nikolai Vatoutin departed with this directive to General HQ for immediate dissemination to the Military Districts. The transmission was completed at 00.30 hours on 22 June 1941.

Chapter 3

Bullets and Bombs

Commando groups of the so-called 'Brandenburg Regiment'* – a Wehrmacht unit that specialized in operations involving disguise – were among the few German units not to hear Hitler's address on the night of 21 June. It was they, who, posing as Red Army officers, were the first to penetrate the Soviet–German border. On the first day of the war the Brandenburgers captured bridges over the Bug, situated along the highway leading to Kiev. Swapping uniforms, insignia, weapons and equipment, they wreaked havoc, seizing numerous bridges, dams and road junctions from the Bug to Pyatigorsk.

The first shots traded on Soviet soil resounded in the dark of night. A group of Brandenburgers, dressed in Red Army uniform, led by Lieutenant Kriegsheim, crossed the border from the Suwałki Salient. Their task was to prevent the destruction of bridges along the Lipsk–Dabrovo road. But the Brandenburgers were spotted and a fierce firefight broke out, in which several border guards were killed. Kriegsheim then attempted to breach the border at an alternative spot. This time he was successful. His was one of many detachments infiltrating the border ahead of the main Wehrmacht forces. Sergeant Vladimir Osaulenko, who began the war in the ranks of the 18th Special Artillery-Machine-Gun Battalion of the Brest Fortified District, recalled:

> As we were walking through the northern garrison at daybreak [22 June], we saw a group of seven or eight soldiers and

---

* Named after their area of recruitment, the 'Brandenburgers' were the special service units of the German Army (the SS had its own special service troops). Dressed and equipped as Red Army soldiers and able to muster a few basic Russian phrases, the Brandenburgers caused mayhem in the opening hours of *Barbarossa*, seizing key objectives such as road and rail bridges.

approached them. They told us that their commander, a Junior Lieutenant, was setting up a combat task for them. A certain captain turned up and yelled: 'What are you talking about, you bastard?' and shot this guy with his pistol. There were many spies and saboteurs. We should have noticed that they were dressed in our new uniform, mainly reserved for captains and majors. They had only a basic stock of [Russian] words. Later they went around riding motorcycles and push-bikes. They were dressed in brand-new stuff – unlike us – so this gave them away on the spot.[1]

At 3.30 a.m. artillery salvoes and the chatter of machine-guns followed the 'quiet' part of the operation.

The main feature of the German assault was the large-scale use of mechanized forces in the first echelon – Panzers leading the advance with motorized units in their wake – designed to maximize the initial 'punch' into Soviet territory. The Germans were able to deliver a devastating opening blow by first concentrating, and then unleashing, a mass of men, machines and materiel against the USSR. In the path of this juggernaut, the Soviet border guards and 'covering' battalions stood no chance.

Four Panzer groups were deployed for *Barbarossa*. Each advanced in two directions, supported by motorized corps in the second echelon. Sometimes, the Germans used so-called 'rollover' tactics, where the Panzers sped through infantry divisions advancing in the first echelon – a similar concept to the Soviet school of thought, which envisioned infantry assaults with supporting armour exploiting gaps or smashing second-line defences. The 'rollover' technique was applied by the 1st Panzer Group during the course of 22 June, but most Panzer units were in the first echelon of the invasion and went straight into action from the outset. The few Soviet battalions facing the onslaught could offer little resistance, so *Barbarossa*'s initial blow struck deep. Nakhman Doushansky, an NKVD officer returning home from vacation by rail, recalls the moment *Barbarossa* began at Siauliai, in the Baltic Special Military District:

We were slowly approaching Siauliai. Suddenly, bombs began falling on the Zhoknya military aerodrome. By the time our train arrived at the station, I had no doubts that war had broken out . . .

I rushed to my house. My half-blind father was standing at the gate waiting for me: 'Nakhman! Take your pistols and run to your comrades! If the Germans come, they'll kill you!' – 'And what about you and Mum?' – 'The Germans won't do us any harm. I was their POW for two years [during the First World War – trans.] and know them well. They're not gonna kill simple people.' [This was a Jewish family and they knew something of the Germans' policy on race – trans.] I'd gone on vacation without firearms, leaving my basic TT pistol in a safe in the department, but I'd hidden two other handguns at home, in a special place. I took the firearms, my leather coat, and some other gear. Then I took my parents to the train station. An evacuation train was already standing on the track, 'under steam'. There was no wild panic at that moment, and I managed to seat my parents in one of the carriages. I said goodbye, jumped onto the tracks, and scrambled onto the last train from Siauliai to Telsiai, on the border. I would never see my kinfolk again. Only my brother, Yakov, survived.

I was not to reach Telsiai that morning. Our train was bombed to pieces near a place called Trishkiai. After this raid I opened the secret packet – the 'mobilization plan' worked out by Morozov for all who worked in my department. Having read it, I understood that our rendezvous point was actually very close to Trishkiai. I walked into town, picked up a horse – minus the saddle – and rode bareback to the supposed meeting place. Artillery rumbled in the west and German planes were permanently overhead. As night fell, NKVD men and border guards began emerging from the forest. Many were wounded, covered in blood, their uniforms filthy and ragged. A few carried trophies captured from the Germans – submachine-guns and rifles. And there I was in a squeaky leather coat without insignia, brand-new blouse and boxcalf boots. The contrast was striking . . .

In 1945 I discovered the fate of my relatives. It seemed that no train left Siauliai for the east on 22 June. Some local

Russian executives had telephoned their superiors to report a mood of 'panic' and 'defeatism'. A detachment of Army 'specialists' arrived and all evacuees were ordered off the train and back to their homes. No one was to leave Siauliai. My parents were later murdered by Lithuanian *Polizei* [i.e. German-controlled militia – ed.] in a ghetto. My youngest brother, Itshak, never made it out of the pioneer camp [a Communist organization for children under 14 years of age – trans.] at Palanga – the circumstances of his death are not known. My sister Rachel and brother Pesakh died trying to reach Russia via Latvia. Lithuanians shot them dead.[2]

Soviet troops stationed in the Baltic republics were simultaneously attacked by two Panzer groups. Pavel Rotmistrov – a future marshal of armoured troops – remembers:

On 21 June, literally hours before the Fascist invasion of Lithuania, the Commander of the Baltic Special Military District, Colonel-General Fedor Kouznetsov arrived at our location. Having hastily entered General Kourkin's office – to whom I was reporting at that moment – Fedor Kouznetsov nodded in reply to our salutes and without further ado announced: 'There is information that a sudden German invasion is likely within the next day or two.' We glanced at each other in silence. Although premonitions of tragedy had plagued us for days, Kouznetsov's statement overwhelmed us. 'And what about the TASS announcement . . ?' asked Alexei Kourkin in a daze. The Commander cut him short: 'In reality that was merely an external policy action and nothing to do with the true military situation.' Kouznetsov – looking haggard and weary – wiped his face with a handkerchief: 'No point discussing these problems now – we've got plenty of our own, which are important enough. Get the corps units out of camp and into the adjacent forests, ready for action. Do it under the pretext of a field drill.' Alexei Kourkin asked for permission to regroup but Kouznetsov declined: 'It's too late for that – German aviation could hit your troops on the march.' My own proposal to evacuate the families of commanders and political officers was also quashed: 'Maybe it's necessary, but we must bear in mind that such a measure would cause panic.'

As soon as Fedor Kouznetsov left, we carried out his directives. Senior staff officers were urgently commandeered to all divisions, in order to help establish observation posts, communications systems, reconnaissance and lines of defence. The Headquarters of Kourkin's 3rd Mechanized Corps departed for Keidany, north of Kaunas. From there we established communications with the 2nd Tank and 84th Motorized Rifle Divisions. We also heard from 11th Army HQ, which informed us that our 5th Tank Division at Alytus was now directly subordinate to the Army Commander.

At 4 a.m. on 22 June 1941 the Luftwaffe executed mass strikes on our aerodromes, rail junctions, sea ports and cities (Riga, Vindava, Libava, Siauliai, Kaunas, Vilnius and Alytus, among others). At the same time, German guns shelled our positions along the border. The rumble of artillery and the thunder of exploding bombs could be heard in Keidany. Between 5.30 and 6 a.m., after a second air raid, enemy troops crossed the border to begin their advance. Between 8.30 and 9 a.m. the Germans threw large mechanized forces into a three-pronged attack: Taurage–Siauliai, Kibartaj–Kaunas, and Kalvaria–Alytus.[3]

When war came, the order of battle for Soviet forces in the Baltic Special Military district was typical of the covering armies – rarefied. The State Border was defended by the 10th Rifle Division plus three-battalion groups from the 5th, 33rd, 90th, 125th and 188th Rifle Divisions. The defence sector adjoining the Baltic was allotted to the 8th Army, commanded by Petr Sobennikov. The 10th Rifle Corps, headed by General-Major Ivan Nikolaev, was situated between Palanga and Sartininkay, covering 8th Army's right flank, but it was thinly stretched. The German Army Group North – which had, by now, fully completed its deployment – enjoyed overwhelming superiority over the opposing covering forces. Each division of the 10th Rifle Corps was attacked by a three-division corps of the German Eighteenth Army: no wonder Nikolaev's troops were quickly dislodged. Palanga, meanwhile, was defended by a single battalion, which was soon surrounded by troops of the German 291st Infantry Division. The Soviet 90th Rifle Division was also rapidly neutralized and partially surrounded, its leader, Colonel Mikhail Goloubev, killed in action.

Meanwhile, a second rifle corps – the 11th, commanded by General-Major Mikhail Shoumilov – was being deployed in a 40km-sector on the 8th Army's left flank. The 125th Division, headed by General-Major Pavel Bogaichuk, took up a defensive line in the first echelon, covering an important stretch of the rail and road route from Tilsit to Siauliai. The 48th Rifle Division – stationed in the Riga area and led by General-Major Pavel Bogdanov – was supposed to bolster the left flank of Bogaichuk's 125th: but the 48th was still en route, formed in marching columns, when the Germans struck, leaving the 125th to defend a 40km-front alone.

On 22 June the 125th Rifle Division faced a serious threat, finding itself in the path of the XXXXI Motorized Corps of 4th Panzer Group. Utilizing their mobility, the Germans took up starting positions just before the invasion began, thus preserving the element of surprise. On the night of 21/22 June, the 1st and 6th Panzer Divisions of XXXXI Corps crossed the Nieman, hitting the border by 3 a.m. Soviet intelligence – judging from local reconnaissance reports – had failed to reveal the presence of the German mechanized group: a typical scenario in the early stages of Barbarossa. Time and again, German mechanized forces foiled Soviet intelligence by executing a forced march to concentrate in a new sector, before delivering a surprise blow. Indeed, the dress rehearsal for future breakthroughs was performed on the first day of the war. Two German Panzer divisions attacked straight off the march after a 5-minute artillery barrage. According to Oberst Ritgen, a veteran of 6th Panzer,

> Enemy resistance in our sector turned out to be much stronger than expected. Our path was obstructed by six anti-tank ditches, covered by infantry and snipers hiding in trees. Fortunately for us, they had no anti-tank artillery or mines. Since none would surrender, we took no prisoners. Nevertheless, our tanks soon ran out of ammo – something that never happened in the Polish and French campaigns.

Replenishment of ammo depended on trucks stuck in a jam somewhere in the rear.[4]

According to Ritgen, not one bridge had been blown to hinder his division's progress, although limited load capacity obliged the German tankmen to ford rivers. Erhard Raus, who commanded a motorized brigade of 6th Panzer, recalled that:

> The artillery shelling began on 22 June 1941 at 3.05 a.m. and soon a signals Storch, sent up as a reconnaissance plane, reported that the wooden machine-gun towers on the outskirts of Siline had been destroyed. After that, the 6th Panzer Division crossed the Soviet border south of Taurage. Combat group 'Von Seckendorf' burst into the village of Siline and quickly mopped up the road to Kangailay. Nevertheless, in a forest east of this place, two Russian companies put up an exceptionally strong fight. Our infantry managed to neutralize the last pocket of resistance only at 16.00 hours, after a fierce action in the forest.
>
> Paying no attention to this obstacle, combat group 'Raus' led the division's advance during those morning hours. We captured a bridge over the River Sesuvis at Kangailay and quickly wiped out scattered enemy groups resisting in the open space around Meskay.
>
> We expected a Russian counter-attack from the northern bank of the Sesuvis but it never materialized. My vanguard units had reached Ertsvilkas [i.e. Erzvilkas – ed.] by nightfall.[5]

Near Erzvilkas, 6th Panzer destroyed marching columns of the 48th Rifle Division. This division, en route from Riga to the border, was badly mauled by powerful air strikes and then assaulted by tanks, sustaining 70 per cent casualties in a single day. But 6th Panzer's immediate task was to reach the River Dubissa and this was not achieved. In the evening, 6th Panzer was attacked by two Soviet bombers – quickly felled by the division's anti-aircraft guns. The division would not reach the Dubissa until 23/24 June.

On 6th Panzer's left flank, 1st Panzer (from the same XXXXI Panzer Corps) also began its advance straight off the march. Advancing along a road, the unit reached the border town of

Taurage by 1 p.m., capturing two bridges across the River Jura. But the action at Taurage turned into a fierce street fight. The place was defended by the 657th Rifle Regiment (125th Rifle Division), commanded by Major Georgievsky. The Germans were forced to fight for possession of every street and house. Eventually, German motorized infantry cleared a path with flamethrowers and explosive charges. By midnight the Soviet defenders had been driven to the north-eastern outskirts of the town. It was typical for the first day of *Barbarossa*: weak resistance during the first hours, gradually stiffening as the main forces of the covering armies were engaged.

The LVI Motorized Corps of the 4th Panzer Group operated in more favourable conditions. It managed to breakthrough almost imperceptibly at the junction between the Soviet 8th and the 11th Armies. The Corps Commander, von Manstein, later wrote:

> On the first day of advance the Corps was supposed to have moved 80km inland in order to capture a bridge across the Dubissa near Airagola. I was familiar with the Dubissa line from First World War days. The sector was a deep river valley with steep banks impassable for tanks. During the Great War our railroad troops built an exemplary wooden bridge across this river in several months. Had the enemy managed to blow up this large bridge near Airagola, the Corps would have had to halt at this line. The enemy would have won time to establish defences on the steep bank opposite, which would have been hard to crush. It was clear that, in this case, there would be no point counting on a sudden capture of the bridges near Dvinsk (Daugavpils). The crossing near Airagola would give us an exceptional springboard for it. No matter how hard the task I set, the 8th Panzer Division, in which I spent most of my time on that day, carried it out. After breaking through the border, subduing the foe's resistance deep in his rear, its vanguard captured the crossing near Airagola by the night of 22 June. The 290th Division followed it at a rapid pace, the 3rd Motorized Infantry Division passed through Memel (Klaipeda) at midday and was sent into combat for a crossing south of Airagola.[6]

The 4th Panzer Group's strike – spearheaded by Manstein's corps – was serious enough for the Soviet Northwestern Front, but its problems were not limited to an incursion by two enemy corps: the Baltic Special Military District had become a window through which two whole Panzer groups could simultaneously smash. The second breakthrough occurred in the Vilnius sector, held by the Soviet 11th Army.

The battle order for Soviet troops in the Vilnius-Kaunas sector was typical: the 5th, 33rd, 188th and 126th Rifle Divisions had only single regiments present at the border, while the 23rd Rifle Division deployed a mere two battalions. This flimsy screen faced the XXVIII, II, V, VIII and XX Corps of the Ninth and Sixteenth Armies, and also the XXXIX and the LVII Motorized Corps of 3rd Panzer Group. Soviet border regiments were thus attacked by at least two infantry divisions each.

During the first days of *Barbarossa*, the German Panzer groups advanced with two motorized corps on the flanks and an Army corps in the centre. The Panzer units pushed deep into Soviet territory, while the infantry mopped up enemy troops caught between the two pincers. This battle order permitted use of local road networks, facilitating a rapid advance, and – as the flanks were covered – reduced the risk of Soviet counterblows. This 'tunnelling' formation was not used in the confined space of the Baltic provinces, but all other Panzer groups (3rd, 2nd and 1st) were deployed in this formation. The external flanks of the 3rd Panzer Group were formed by the XXXIX and LVII Motorized Corps, and the centre by the infantry of V Army Corps. The spearhead of XXXIX Motorized Corps was pointed at the crossing over the Neman near Alytus, and the 12th Panzer Division of the LVII Corps moved towards the river crossing near Merkine. The XXXIX Corps was supposed to make its way to Alytus with 7th Panzer covered from the north (the left flank) by 20th Panzer, and from the south (the right flank) by the 20th Motorized Division. This formation illustrates some apprehension on the part of Germans – the strong flank cover was supposed to safeguard the crack group from counter-attacks by Soviet rifle and tank units. It is also noteworthy that most mobile troops of Hoth's Panzer Group remained in the rear. The 19th

Panzer Division and the 14th and 18th Motorized Divisions were waiting for their moment to come. But the precaution turned out to be unnecessary, for no counterblows occurred during the first hours of the war. The Germans immediately drilled into the Soviet 11th Army to a considerable depth. Hoth later wrote:

> The commanding officers of the 39th Panzer Corps sent both tank regiments and a part of the 20th Motorized Division along the Suwałki–Kalvaria motorway with the aim of capturing heights south of Kalvaria, which had important tactical value. Those forces were excessive, and such an outlay was not justifying itself.[7]

German Intelligence's numerical assessment of Soviet troops in the Vilnius sector appeared strongly exaggerated. It was not too difficult to dislodge scattered screens of individual battalions at the border and bypass larger units. Having outflanked the 128th Rifle Division from north and south, both motorized corps of the 3rd Panzer Group advanced rapidly. Having begun the offensive at 3.05 a.m. a motorized brigade of the 7th Panzer Division was approaching Kalvaria 5 hours later, at 8 a.m. Alytus and the bridges over the Neman were the next target. After the commencement of hostilities the main forces of the 5th, 23rd and 188th Rifle Divisions pushed towards the border, getting entangled with the enemy southwest of Kaunas, while the main axis of the German advance went unchecked. Meanwhile, the only Soviet unit standing between the Germans and Alytus was the 5th Tank Division – the strongest and, more importantly, most mobile reserve available to 11th Army. Had there been sufficient manpower to contain the initial German strike at the border, this reserve division might have counter-attacked in support of the rifle units: now it found itself under attack. At 4.20 a.m. German aircraft hit depots, barracks and an aerodrome in 5th Tank Division's vicinity – fortunately, most men and equipment had already relocated to field camps, but the air raid dispelled any doubts that the war had actually begun. Fedorov, the divisional commander, ordered his units to prepare for action, and sent a vanguard detachment – several tanks and companies of motorized infantry – to dig in on the left bank of the Neman. Why had defensive positions not been dug already? Because the situation that was unfolding had not been foreseen – indeed, the division might have reasonably expected to be counter-attacking the Raseiniai area, rather than defending the Neman. The bridges across the Neman had been prepared for demolition by the 4th Pioneer Regiment of the Baltic Special Military District, and according to Hoth: 'A captured officer of engineers informed us that he'd been ordered to blow up the Alytus bridges at 13.00 hours.' But this did not occur – possibly due to the intervention of the Brandenburgers. Thus, the bridges were still intact on 22 June and German motorized units were able to cross to the east bank of the Neman. Next day, however, when VI Corps reached the river, the Germans found the bridges belatedly destroyed.

Units of the 7th Panzer Division, advancing towards the Neman, encountered Fedorov's vanguard detachment but quickly brushed it aside. The Germans secured both the northern and southern bridges near Alytus and were soon on the eastern bank. There, for the first time, the Germans encountered the Soviet T-34 tank. One T-34, in position near the bridge, immediately knocked out a PzKpfw38(t), which had just crossed the river. And although the German tank crews returned fire with their 37mm cannon, the weapon proved ineffective against Soviet armour. A veteran of the Soviet 5th Tank Division later recalled:

> Our division approached the eastern bank of the Neman several days before Barbarossa – in time to take up defensive positions. I was appointed messenger between Divisional HQ and the 5th ATB [Auto-Transport Battalion – trans.]. At 4.20 a.m. on 22 June, we heard buzzing engines – the bombing of the military camp had begun. At the same time, the Chief of Staff, Major Belikov, ordered me to head off to the western part of the city, to find out what was on fire. We were met by a column of civilians, which parted as our motorcycle drove through at full speed. But after we had passed, they [i.e. unidentified persons from the civilian column – ed.] started shooting at us with sub-machine guns, and as we arrived at our barracks, they shot up our motorcycle.

About 11.30 a.m., a bedraggled woman was escorted to HQ, having swum the Neman. She said that German tanks were beyond the city, but the Public Prosecutor screamed: 'She's a spy!' and shot her dead. Thirty minutes later, near the bridge, soldiers detained a Lithuanian man who told us, in broken Russian, that German tanks had entered the city. A Military Police officer called him a 'provocateur', pulled out a pistol, and shot him. At that moment, our flak gunners opened up at German aircraft, and our artillery batteries put up a concentrated barrage – but it was too late.

We came across one of our tanks and knocked on the hatch. A tanker opened up and we told him that German tanks were nearby, on the road next to us, but he replied that he had no armour-piercing shells. We approached a second tank and found the platoon commander, who immediately ordered: 'Follow me!' And two or three tanks plunged out of the bushes and into the approaching German Panzers, shooting on the move. Without losing a single vehicle, they destroyed half a dozen German tanks – ramming them off the road and into the ditch. Then they rushed over the bridge to the western bank of the river, immediately running into more German armour. An enemy tank went up in flames, then one of ours. After that, I saw only smoke, amid the rumble of explosions and the grating clank of metal.[8]

Although German units had successfully crossed the Neman and established bridgeheads on the eastern bank, they were unable to break out due to fire from Soviet tanks. That said, Fedorov's 5th Tank Division failed to annihilate the attackers and, as evening fell, an uneasy stalemate reigned. By 7.30 p.m., elements of the 20th Panzer Division of XXXIX Motorized Corps moved up to the bridges – passing much-needed ammunition to their comrades in 7th Panzer. Reinforced and replenished – and supported by artillery – the Germans resumed the offensive, breaking out of the northern bridgehead and working their way into the rear of those Soviet units pinning the southern bridgehead. Next day, the Germans reached Vilnius. Fedorov's losses at Alytus were heavy: 16 T-28 tanks (out of 24), 27 T-34s (out of 44), 30 BT-7s (out of 45).

The scenario described above was typical of 22 June: a speedy German breakthrough at the border, slowing down in the face of stiffer resistance, only to resume as mobile units outflanked the defenders. Junior Sergeant Sergei Matsapoura, a gunlayer in the Soviet 126th Division, remembers:

> We soon found ourselves firing at the Fascist infantry from maximum range. As soon as a salvo of shells had been fired, the command came: 'Stop! Record the settings.' That morning, at Lieutenant Komarov's battery, I first heard a phrase that would be repeated time and again: 'Spare the ammunition!' The border was west of us, but by noon we were firing in a southerly direction. I remember that because the midday sun shone straight into the barrel of my cannon. The fact that our battery had swung first south, and then southeast, meant only one thing: the Fascists had penetrated deep into Soviet territory.[9]

By the evening of 22 June, troops of the Soviet 11th Army, deployed near the border, had been encircled or scattered. But the impending disaster had been anticipated early in the day. At 9.35 a.m., the commander of the Soviet Northwestern Front reported to Moscow: 'Large [enemy] forces of tanks and motorized troops are forcing their way towards Druskeniki. The 128th Rifle Division has been encircled – there is no accurate information regarding its situation . . .'. His report concluded with the following assessment:

> The 184th Rifle Division (which has not been brought up to full strength yet and is completely unreliable) is camped at Orany; the 179th Rifle Division at Svencionys is also undermanned and unreliable, as is the 181st Rifle Division at Gulbene; while the 183rd Rifle Division is on the march to the Riga camp. For these reasons, I am unable to create a force to deal with the breakthrough on my left flank . . .[10]

Meanwhile, as armoured and mechanized units belonging to Army Group Centre's 3rd Panzer Group overran the Baltic Special Military District (Northwestern Front), infantry divisions of the German Ninth Army launched an attack from the Suwałki Salient, striking into the rear of Red Army units stationed in the Białystok area.

The roar of powerful artillery tractors was heard on the Soviet side of the border near Grodno, as fourteen super-heavy artillery batteries attached to the German VIII Army Corps took post. The mightiest instrument of this 'orchestra' was the 24cm KZ 'Petersdorf' cannon, which fired 150kg shells up to a distance of 37km. A report logged by VIII Corps HQ stated that its artillery 'performed a successful reveille for the Grodno garrison', adding that 'infantrymen accommodated in the barracks must have incurred heavy losses'. Thus, Soviet soldiers stationed around Grodno fell victim to the most advanced system of armament.

The Soviet 56th Rifle Division, commanded by General–Major Mikhail Sakhno, had taken up its assigned position on the perimeter of the Suwałki Salient in good time, but was outnumbered by the attackers and dismembered. Lazar Belkin, a graduate of the Gomel Rifle Machine-gun School (GSPU), recalls how the 56th Rifle Division fought on the first day of the war:

> I had been appointed to the Belorussian Special Military District, to the 3rd Army, 56th Rifle Division. On 21 June, we ten young Red Army officers, graduates of the GSPU, arrived at Grodno. By the evening of the same day, we were already at Gozhi, on the Polish border, where our 184th Rifle Regiment was stationed. As the regimental commander had gone to Moscow, we were received by the Chief of Staff, who glanced at our papers before waving us off: 'It's late, go to bed. See, there's an empty tent over there. We'll sort things out with you in the morning.'
>
> In the fifth hour of the morrow we were woken by the buzz of aircraft. We gathered at the HQ tent – dozens of planes droning overhead, heading east. To be frank, no one was yet thinking about war: we assumed these were manoeuvres – either ours or German – and we quietly walked to the river to wash. Moments later, German planes attacked our camp – the regiment lost at least 60 per cent killed or wounded in this first raid.
>
> We returned to where our tent had been – everything was mixed with soil and blood. I found my jackboots, someone's breeches, but could not find my blouse and shoulder-belt.

We'd gone to the river in shorts and vests, so I threw on a civilian jacket – I lacked the nerve to strip a dead soldier. Only now did we understand: this is war. At midday we were officially informed hostilities had begun.

Panic struck after the air raid. I was ordered to take charge of a machine-gun platoon from Sergeant Kachkaev, who was with two 'Maxims' on the regiment's right flank. But Kachkaev was nowhere to be found – vanished, along with his machine-guns and their crews. What was left of the regiment took up a defensive position and remained in place for almost a week, but no one touched us – no sign of any Germans in front. The regiment was mostly manned by recruits – Poles from West Belorussia, who dispersed to their homes during the first days of fighting. The panic was indescribable. There were no communications with divisional HQ. We were shrouded in uncertainty, with no idea we'd been encircled and were now deep in the enemy's rear.

Five days later, a German *rama* [i.e. 'frame', the Russian nickname for the twin-fuselage, twin-engine FW-189 reconnaissance aeroplane – trans.] circled our location. Shortly after, Germans roared up on motorcycles, dismounted, and went into the attack. We received them with heavy fire and pushed them back. During this action, one of our platoon commanders managed to outflank the Germans, taking six of them prisoner. These POWs were unlike the Germans described to us at school – strong, sun-tanned, collars unbuttoned, sleeves rolled up. We questioned them, and I translated, knowing some German. They all answered in the same manner: 'Stalin kaput! Moskva kaput! Russiche Schwein!' We warned them: give us information or you'll be shot. Still the same answers. We shot them one at a time but none caved in. They faced death firmly, like real fanatics. Later that same evening a liaison officer reached us, telling us that Minsk had fallen and that we were in a pocket. He ordered us to quit and try to break out in small groups. One guy silently turned around and left on his own – perhaps to surrender.

Being already on the other side of the old border, we called at a nearby village, asking for food. Local women told us the Germans were camped on the other side of the village. The girls then brought us civilian clothes and bread, before walking us to the dairy farm. But the supervisor tried to drive us away: 'You Stalinist degenerates! Filthy Komsomol bastards! We've had no life because of you! I won't give you milk – I'd rather give it to the Germans.' I replied: 'Why are you yelling at us, Red Army soldiers? We are all Soviet people aren't we? Shame on you! Come to your senses!' Mad with hatred and screaming obscenities, the man grabbed a scythe and scurried towards me, but his daughter dragged him to the ground. 'So long, scumbag!' I said as we left. What did I expect? After all, the war had only just begun and there seemed little chance of surviving the German encirclement.[11]

The 213th Rifle Regiment (56th Division) fought alongside the 184th. Its commander, Major Timofei Yakovlev, suggested crossing the Neman near the village of Gozhi, together with units from the 9th and 10th Detached Machine-gun Battalions. His plan was to push north-east through woodland towards the front line. On 26 June, during a fierce action, Yakovlev's scratch force crossed the Neman and moved towards Druskeniki, where they endured a further desperate battle as losses mounted. According to Sultan Asketkhanov, a former cadet with the 213th, prisoners, vehicles and weapons were all lost to the enemy, although the regimental banner was preserved by Senior Sergeant Komissarov, a native of Orekhovo-Zuevo, near Moscow. Meanwhile, the eastward trek to the front line continued with the Germans in hot pursuit. Yakovlev's force fought several skirmishes, losing more men and equipment. Timofei Yakovlev himself was wounded and captured. His namesake, Leonid Yakovlev, a former clerk in the 213th, remembers his commander's last hours in a German POW camp:

He was bony, beaten, in threadbare clothes, wounded, but still in uniform. In bidding his final farewell, he assured us of the inevitable victory over the Fascists: 'Don't succumb before the enemy. Fight on and strive, whoever you are, wherever you are, and no matter how!' These were his last words to us as we were driven away with kicks from German jackboots. Later, we heard they shot him . . .[12]

The defenders could only hope to contain the German advance for a time. Particular doggedness was displayed by pillbox garrisons in the Grodno Fortified District. According to the desptach written by the commander of the German 28th Infantry Regiment:

> As to the Sopotskino sector and north of it [. . .] the matter of concern is the enemy's decision to stand firm at any cost. Here, the principles guiding our advance did not bring success. The pillboxes could only be destroyed by powerful explosives and we lacked sufficient means to tackle so many installations [. . .] The garrisons hid in the lower levels during our attacks. It was impossible to capture them in there [. . .] As soon as the assault groups rolled back, the enemy would revive again and man their guns.[13]

Some garrisons resisted for several days, by which time the front line had rolled way past the border.

The 56th Rifle Division's collapse made the commander of 3rd Army undertake urgent measures to restore the integrity of the front. The 11th Mechanized Corps was a mobile reserve under 3rd Army command. But communications between 3rd Army HQ and the District HQ had been severed by the German air raid on Volkovysk at 4 p.m., so the 11th Mechanized moved up to the Grodno–Sokółka–Indura area, in accordance with the prearranged Soviet battle plan. German infantry encountered T-34 tanks near Grodno. The Soviet 29th Tank Division, led by Colonel Nikolai Stoudnev, had been stationed near Grodno before the war, and so found itself in the path of the German VIII Army Corps. The 29th Tank Division began the war with just sixty-six tanks, including two KVs and twenty-six T-34s – the remainder consisted of T-26s of various modifications. The division deployed under enemy air strikes, reaching its starting positions by 8 p.m., when a reconnaissance battalion was pushed up to the August Canal. After mustering south-west of Grodno, the division received a directive from General Vasili Kouznetsov:

In order to provoke conflict and drag the Soviet Union into war, the enemy has infiltrated the State Border with saboteur gangs and bombed some of our cities. I order the 29th Tank Division, in cooperation with the 4th Rifle Corps, to annihilate the enemy in the Sopotskin–Kalety area – but the border must not be crossed. Report to me on completion.[14]

The wording of Vasili Kouznetsov's order shows an unwillingness – even at this late stage – to accept that full-blown war had broken out. Also, by referring to 'gangs', it would appear the scale of the German invasion was still unknown to Vasili Kouznetsov, despite the fact that regular Wehrmacht units were already on Soviet soil.

Later, the 29th Tank Division received a specific task from the commander of the 11th Mechanized Corps, in which he demanded the destruction of German units advancing on the Sopotskin–Lipsk front. At the same time, Colonel Mikhail Panov, commanding the 33rd Tank Division, was ordered to advance in the direction of Lipsk–Augustów. Thus, by committing his mobile reserves, Vasili Kouznetsov interrupted the German infantry advance (in the following days, the deployment of 6th Mechanized Corps would force German foot-sloggers onto the defensive). But this local success came at a price: by the close of 22 June, Nikolai Stoudnev's 29th Tank Division had virtually ceased to exist, having lost most of its armour.

Photo Album:
Barbarossa Unleashed

Viacheslav Molotov signing the Treaty of Non-Aggression between Germany and the Soviet Union, Moscow, 23 August 1939.

Supreme Commander Josef Stalin, Narkom of Foreign affairs Viacheslav Molotov, and Narkom of Defence Kliment Voroshilov (replaced by Semen Timoshenko on the eve of war).

A border guard patrol.

A soldier's band. On the wall next to the portrait of Stalin is a poster saying: 'Be honest in front of the Party . . . learn the programme and tactics of the Party.'

The last days of peace:
an infantry senior
lieutenant (on the left)
and an Air Force junior
lieutenant (note the
'chicken' emblem on
his sleeve) in a
Crimean sanatorium.

Studying the T-26 tank,
Military Academy of
Motorization and
Mechanization,
summer 1940. Note
that the cadets are
highly decorated.

BT-7 tanks, model
1937, which made
up the bulk of the
Red Army's
mechanized corps
units' combat power,
are seen here on
parade in Moscow, 1
May 1941.

Students from one of Minsk's universities. Note the black 'plate' on the wall—a radio transmitter. These were never turned off, so most people heard Molotov's speech via this device, which became one of the symbols of the 1941 catastrophe.

A pre-war propaganda poster featuring Narkom of Defence, Kliment Voroshilov.

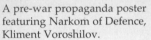

Moscow, May 1941.

Moscow VDNKh, 1941.

On the border a
few hours
before the war.

Goebbels announcing
the war on the
morning of 22 June
1941.

German soldiers crossing the border.

Hitler's proclamation to the German soldiers.

The first POWs.

The first POWs –
some are not even
dressed.

A Jewish junior
commander.

The first German
casualties.

First bombs
dropped on the
Soviet Union.

In the navigator's
cabin of an
He-111.

A radio
loudspeaker placed
on a Russian street.

Soviet people
listen to
Molotov's speech
on 22 June.

The people of Leningrad hear
Molotov's speech.

Volunteers enlisting for the Red Army.

'Our cause is just. The enemy will be destroyed.
Victory will be ours.'

On the way to the front.

A Maxim machine-gun crew firing at the enemy.

A T-28 heavy
tank crew
receiving a task.

A peasant gives milk
to a wounded soldier.

Loading the
gun.

Infantry on the
march. The soldier
in the centre closest
to the camera
carries a box
containing
magazines for a DP
light machine-gun.

Two captains of
the medical service
help a wounded
German soldier.

Attack support by
a BT light tank.

A staged photo of a captured Bf-109.

An infantry attack.

Infantry riding a T-26 into battle.

Attack! The soldier in front is armed with an SVT semi-automatic rifle.

Chapter 4

Brest: the Rat Trap

In Belorussia, the worst possible sequence of events occurred around the Brest Citadel – a large fortress dating from the nineteenth century.* The core of the fortress was located on an island washed by the Rivers Bug and Muchawiec. It consisted of a red-brick, two-storey, ring-shaped barrack, 1.8km long, with 500 rooms, capable of accommodating 12,000 soldiers. Storage facilities were located beneath these rooms or casements, and beneath the stores lay a network of tunnels. There were two gates connecting the Citadel with bridges across the Muchawiec. A third gate led to a bridge across the main channel of the Western Bug. A system of river channels and canals formed three islands on which the Terespol, Volyn and Kobrin forts were situated. In 1941, these islands were known locally as Frontier Island, Hospital Island and the Northern Island, respectively. The Germans referred to them by geographical location: Western, Southern and Northern. Enclosing this cluster of forts was an earthwork some 10m high. And yet, in August 1940, the Brest Citadel made a poor impression on the 4th Army's Chief of Staff, Leonid Sandalov:

> The outer wall of the Citadel and the external earth rampart, surrounded by water obstacles, would place the troops located inside in a precarious situation. After all, only a single rifle battalion plus supporting artillery was allocated for the

---

* Designed in 1830 by the Russian General, Karl Opperman, the Brest Citadel was constructed between 1836 and 1842 with later additions. Captured by the Germans in 1915, the fortress was granted to Poland following the Treaty of Riga in 1921. During the German invasion of Poland, the Citadel held out for four days against Guderian's XIX Panzer Corps. In September 1939, following the Ribbentrop-Molotov Pact and Stalin's subsequent invasion of Poland, the Citadel reverted to Russian control.

defence of the Citadel itself, according to the plans of the District. The rest of the garrison was supposed to quit the Citadel quickly and take up positions still being constructed along the border; but the carrying capacity of the gates was too small: it would have taken at least three hours to evacuate the Citadel.[1]

In other words, the Brest Citadel was a rat trap.

According to the pre-war Soviet battle plan, the 4th Army, under General-Major Alexander Korobkov, stationed near Brest, was supposed to support elements of the 6th and 42nd Rifle Divisions, which, prior to the outbreak of hostilities, occupied the Brest Citadel. Furthermore, the 100th Rifle Division, stationed at Minsk, would, according to the plan, advance to the border by rail on the *third day* of mobilization. In other words, the Soviet Command, hampered by a First World War mindset, was not prepared for the speed and ferocity of the German onslaught.

Standing in the path of Army Group Centre and dominating crossings over the Bug, as well as the main Warsaw–Moscow road and rail links, Brest was a major German objective. Considering the Citadel a tough nut to crack, its capture was delegated to some 20,000 troops drawn from the 31st, 34th and 45th Infantry Divisions, while the XXXVII and XXIV Motorized Corps struck north and south of the city. The Germans also deployed powerful artillery, rocket mortars, flame-throwers and tear gas.

Meanwhile, news of *Barbarossa* had passed, like an electric shock, from the German deserter Liskow all the way to Moscow. At midnight, 21/22 June, General-Major Alexander Korobkov and his chief of staff, Leonid Sandalov, were summoned to Army HQ, along with other Army and department chiefs. As no directives had been issued via the District HQ – apart from a general 'high alert' order – Alexander Korobkov took it upon himself to order distribution of the sealed envelopes containing the pre-arranged battle instructions to all units. But a fateful delay occurred when, around 2 a.m., the cable connecting Army HQ and the District troops failed. The line was restored around 3.30 a.m. (breaks were detected at Zaprudy and Zhabinka) – too late for Korobkov's initiative to pay off. Meanwhile, with the minutes counting down to

Barbarossa, General Dmitri Pavlov, commander of the Western Special Military District, signalled units to prepare for action. Dmitri Pavlov also demanded that the 42nd Rifle Division evacuate the Brest Citadel 'in parcels', while the 14th Mechanized Corps deployed for combat. Air assets were to relocate to field aerodromes. But the instructions were belated – as were the telephone calls from Alexander Korobkov to Major Sherbakov, the 42nd Rifle Division's chief of staff, urging him to quit the Citadel and make for the assembly area: Sherbakov had barely managed to gather his unit commanders, with a view to issuing Korobkov's commands, when German artillery began to rumble. Furthermore, the divisional commander, General-Major Ivan Lazarenko, was yet to be located and informed that war had broken out.

By 4.20 a.m., Sherbakov was reporting to 4th Army HQ that the Citadel was under heavy artillery fire. Staff officers understood the significance: the rat trap had shut. And yet, the situation was somewhat smoothed by the fact that several battalions from the 6th and 42nd Rifle Divisions had already been pulled from the Citadel for training. Thus, when the fighting began, the Citadel would be defended by 3,500 military personnel plus their families and some medical staff. The first enemy strike was described in the following combat dispatch of the 6th Rifle Division:

> At 4 a.m. on 22 June a hurricane of fire was unleashed on barracks and buildings housing commanding officers. This barrage brought confusion and panic. Those commanders who survived the bombardment of their accommodation blocks were prevented from making their way to the centre of the Citadel by heavy fire raining down on the gates and bridges. As a result, soldiers and NCOs, left without orders, quit the Citadel alone or in small groups – some still undressed – under the enemy's fire. It was impossible to estimate losses, as uncoordinated mobs from the 6th and 42nd Divisions mingled together, unable to reach the muster ground, which, since 6 a.m., had been targeted by concentrated artillery fire.[2]

Shells were not only raining on the barracks – the whole complex was gripped by a murderous bombardment, trapping troops inside and forcing them on to the defensive. Meanwhile, any artillery pieces, vehicles or horses left in the Citadel's open parks were wiped out.

Although the Germans already had experience of storming the Brest Citadel during the Polish campaign of 1939, only 210mm howitzers (21cm Moerser 18) and rocket mortars were initially deployed against the tough old fortress and, despite the impressive pyrotechnical effect, their shells failed to pierce the thick walls. While this fire squall wiped out every living creature in the fortress yard, garrison troops hiding in the casements managed to survive. The barrage was witnessed by German infantrymen lining the riverbank, awaiting the order to assault (they'd only been allotted 8 hours for the task), and to them it seemed nothing could survive such a deluge of fire. But inside the fortress civilians (including children) were patching up wounded soldiers and scurrying after whatever food and ammo could be salvaged from the blazing depots. In other words, once the defenders recovered from the initial shock, resistance began to stiffen – as the German foot-sloggers would find to their cost. The situation is described in the German 45th Division's official history:

Inside the Citadel, the action acquired an unforeseen character. Several hours after our entry, the Corps Command had to commit elements of the 133rd Infantry Regiment. Soon, all the division's reserves were thrown into the attack. Our losses – especially in officers – quickly reached a deplorable level.[3]

The historian of the 45th Division, Rudolph Gschöpf, recorded the following action at the Terespol fort, in the first hour of fighting:

Numerous 'cuckoos' [slang term for snipers in trees – trans.] and camouflaged fighters on the Western Island were preventing our reinforcements getting through. Already, on the first day of the invasion, the HQs of the 3rd Battalion, 135th Infantry Regiment and the 1st Battalion, 99th Artillery Regiment, had been destroyed, the commanders killed.[4]

Most of the Soviet defenders on the 'Western Island' were border guards. At 10.50 a.m., the HQ of the German 45th Division reported: 'The Russians are putting up stiff resistance. Inside the

Citadel, the enemy has organized an infantry defence, supported by some forty tanks and armoured vehicles. Fire from enemy snipers has led to heavy losses among our officers and NCOs.'

By 2.30 p.m., General-Lieutenant Fritz Schlieper, commander of the 45th Division, had practically given up on the central part of the Citadel, opting to withdraw those units that had penetrated the Soviet defences under cover of darkness. Such a move would give the German artillery a free hand, allowing them to resume their bombardment – except for the fact that some seventy Germans, who had captured a church (converted into a social club), were effectively trapped within their hard-won prize. Thus the German assault, which was supposed to take 8 hours, lasted eight days.* Guderian, commander of the 2nd Panzer Group wrote: 'The garrison of the important Brest Citadel defended especially fiercely, holding out for several days, having barred the roads and railway over the West Bug to the Muchawiec.'

Fig. 4: Table showing Fortified Districts of the Western Special military District.

FORTIFIED DISTRICT	FRONTAGE (Kilometres)	CENTRES OF DEFENCE	PILLBOXES		
			Under construction	Completed	Operational
Grodnensky (68)	80	9	606	98	42
Osovetsky (66)	60	8	594	59	35
Zambrovsky (64)	70	10	550	53	30
Bretsky (62)	120	10	380	128	49

However, while the Brest garrison heroically defied the German attack, failure to place the 6th and 42nd Rifle Divisions in their allocated border sectors had serious consequences, with the burden of defence falling on units of the Brest Fortified District. Sergeant Vladimir Osaulenko of the 18th Special Machine-Gun Battalion (62nd Brest Fortified District), recalls the night of 21/22 June:

---

* Several days into the siege, the Germans deployed 540mm artillery and two 600mm guns, capable of firing concrete-piercing shells weighing over 2 tonnes. The Citadel fell on 30 June, following a concerted infantry assault. Previous to this, a failed attempt to break out had weakened the garrison. Those defenders who survived spent the rest of the war in German concentration camps.

That night I was on duty as battery orderly, having sent most of the guys to a dance in town, where we used to meet up with girls. Half an hour later the commander of our 1st Battery turned up: 'What's going on? Get your guys back where they should be, and tell them that on Monday we begin stocking the pillboxes with food and ammo.' When the guys returned, my buddy, a Ukrainian called Reshetilo, said: 'Volodya, my girlfriend told me something . . .' – 'What did she say?' – 'She said that tomorrow will be bad for us . . .' – 'Oh yeah, why?' – 'She said the war will begin tomorrow.' I thought that, although some girl thinks the war will start, our commanders remain silent – she must be wrong. But around midnight, a train left for Germany . . .

Then, around 2 a.m., one of the cooks appeared: 'Hey, Volodya, the water's turned off in the kitchen – I can't cook breakfast!' Ten minutes later he pops up again: 'Now the power's off!' At that moment I knew the girl was right. About 3.30 a.m. we heard the heavy buzz of aircraft overhead – flying east over our territory. It was war!

I ran to the HQ building, expecting to find an officer – no one there. I grabbed the phone, thinking to call the chief of staff – the line was dead. I ran to the barrack block, shouting: 'Battle alarm! Grab your weapons and take post according the battle order!' Then, as the last soldiers stumbled out of the barracks, a terrific rumble was heard – the Germans had 600mm cannon trained on the Citadel. Imagine the sound they made!

The first minutes of the attack – utter confusion. The bridge from Brest to Terespol had not been demolished and the Germans poured across. About an hour later they turned up at the checkpoint, 100m in front of our barracks. Our guys were still drowsy but coped pretty well. A unit occupied trenches in front of the fort, firing from rifles and machine-guns. Another unit defended the HQ building. Meanwhile, I manned one of several machine-guns set up in the mess. When a German armoured vehicle showed up, we made short work of it, knocking it out with grenades and machine-gun fire as it entered the checkpoint. Then, nine enemy planes – JU87s – appeared and dived on our trenches: not a single soldier survived that raid.

Just after that, we realized the Germans had begun to encircle us. What's more, we were running out of ammo. And so I ordered a withdrawal under covering fire. Back then, no one had a watch, so I guess we'd been fighting for over two hours. We decided to make a dash for the Northern garrison – me and a guy called Chizh, from the 3rd Battery, were the first to make the attempt. Straightaway, shooting started – we tumbled and crawled our way forward and made it. But the forty or fifty guys we left behind, without a commander, suddenly stampeded like a herd of cattle – the Germans opened up a massive fire from automatic weapons. None of our guys got across. The war was only three hours old and only two men from the Special Battalion remained alive.[5]

Other units fared little better, deploying from their barracks under enemy fire. A platoon commander of the 18th Special Anti-Tank Artillery Battalion recalls:

We had to man the pillboxes under fire, which caused heavy casualties. Out of eighteen soldiers and NCOs in my platoon, only five actually made it to a pillbox. The men had to crawl to the depot for food and ammo during combat – that is, until it was blown up. But we stood firm for the rest of that day, stubborn fire being laid down by pillboxes under Junior Lieutenants Moskvin, Orekhov and Glinin . . .[6]

Despite such heroics, failure to deploy the full force of the 6th and 42nd Rifle Divisions ensured local successes were shortlived. In the event, Guderian's 2nd Panzer Group pushed forward, crossing the Bug and reaching the River Lesna by 10.30 a.m. A little after midday, the 18th Panzer Division encountered the Soviet 30th Tank Division, which was en route for the border. But Colonel Semen Bogdanov (future commander of the 2nd Guards Tank Army), had only T-26s at his disposal and could do little more than hinder the German advance.

South of Brest, Model's 3rd Panzer Division crossed the Bug without difficulty, as the breakdown in Soviet communications meant the 75th Rifle Division was left without orders till after 4 a.m.: by which time it had already suffered losses from German artillery and aviation. Brest itself was soon skewered between two steel torrents, as German motorized units manoeuvred north and south – only the waterlogged terrain hindering their progress.

As for the Soviet 22nd Tank Division (14th Mechanized Corps) – camped on flat ground in Brest's southern military station, a mere 3km from the State Border – it, too, was bombed and shelled without warning, sustaining heavy losses in men and equipment. The situation turned hellish when the division's fuel and ammo depots exploded, igniting an inferno. Nevertheless, the battle alarm was sounded, heralding a move on Zhabinka, east of Brest, in accordance with the pre-arranged defence plan. Thus, by 8 a.m., the division – lacking many of its tanks, vehicles and artillery – found itself conducting a disorderly passage of the Muchawiec at Pugachevo, south-east of Brest, in an effort to reach Zhabinka as soon as possible.

In the Kiev Special Military District, the advance units of Mikhail Potapov's 5th Army were some 40km from the River Bug when *Barbarossa* began. Around 6 a.m. the alarm went up and the rifle regiments began their advance to the border, hampered by enemy air raids. At 7 a.m., following Germany's official declaration of war against the USSR, Moscow issued Directive No. 2, instructing Red Army units to 'attack the enemy with all means and destroy him in those areas where he has violated the Soviet border'. The directive also authorized bombing raids up to 150km inside German territory. But once again, Soviet troops received their orders too late for effective execution. For example, the 99th Rifle Division received permission to deploy its artillery as late as 10 a.m. on 22 June.

Between 11 a.m. and 1 p.m., the 87th and 124th Rifle Divisions encountered the vanguard of Reichenau's Sixth Army. It was too late to occupy defensive lines, so Soviet troops went into combat off the march, putting up a serious fight and counter-attacking in places. But there was no solid front line to protect the flanks of these rifle regiments, making them vulnerable to encirclement.

Advance elements of the 87th Rifle Division arrived at the southern outskirts of Vladimir-Volynsky by 9 a.m. and were soon in combat with the German 298th Infantry Division. As the rest of the 87th Rifle Division moved up, the Commander, General Alyaboushev, decided to counter-attack. The 96th Rifle Regiment, supported by the 212th Howitzer Artillery Regiment, advanced from the south-western side of Vladimir-Volynsky, striking for the Bug south of Ustilug. The 16th Rifle Regiment of Colonel Filimonov, supported by the 178th Artillery Regiment, advanced from the north-western side of Vladimir-Volynsky, aiming to capture Ustilug and push beyond it to the banks of the Western Bug. This attack was supported by two battalions from the 41st Tank Division. During the day, the 87th Rifle Division managed to push the Germans back some 10km west of Vladimir-Volynsky.

But while the division was advancing to Ustilug, the situation in its own defence sector was steadily deteriorating. At 1 p.m., the 14th Panzer Division, having crossed the Bug, went into action, tipping the scales in the Germans' favour. Meanwhile, a 20km-gap had opened between the Soviet 87th Rifle Division and the 124th Rifle Division. German troops poured through this gap, overwhelming border guards and scattered pillboxes, and flanking Alyaboushev's 87th Rifle Division. Despite fierce Soviet resistance along the 'Molotov Line', by the evening of the 22nd, German infantry had penetrated as far as the railway line linking Vladimir-Volynsky and Sokal. Konstantin Malygin, Chief of Staff of the 41st Tank Division, recalls the sequence of events between 21/22 June near Vladimir-Volynsky:

> I had planned to go fishing with Colonel Vasil'ev on Sunday 22 June. On the Saturday night I went to bed early, as I'd have to be up before dawn. But I couldn't sleep. I felt uneasy somehow – worrying about my understaffed division. Eventually I dropped off and was awoken by the door bell: 'Get up fisherman!' called Vasil'ev, 'You're gonna sleep past daybreak!' I jumped out of bed and rang HQ – they said all was quiet, no directives had been received. I told them: 'If anything happens, ring me at the polygon [i.e. military training ground or exercise field – trans.], I'll be with Colonel Vasil'ev.'

We drove towards the border, where the polygon was situated, almost on the banks of the Luga, which flows into the Bug. Dawn was bleeding crimson across the sky; villages, fields and woods were shrouded in the haze – sleeping peacefully in the still air. 'The fishing will be good today!' Vasil'ev smiled and turned to our driver, 'What do you reckon, Kolya?' But the guy muffled the engine and asked in turn, 'What's that?' Flares soared, red and green, from over the border. This was followed by the rumble of distant thunder. Suddenly, flashes of tracer flew overhead. 'Turn back!' I yelled at the driver – half-imagining this might be some kind of exercise by the 5th Army, which we tankers knew nothing about. But as the air burst with bullets and bombs all doubt fled – it was war!

Having thrown away our fishing rods we rushed to the garrison, flocks of German aircraft flying above us at varying altitudes. The lower group formed a circle and, diving one after the other, bombed the military station at Vladimir-Volynsky with screaming sirens – deafening and blood-chilling. Explosions followed one upon the other. Someone on the outskirts of town – a traitor or saboteur – kept sending red flares towards our depots, indicating targets for the attackers.

The alarm had already been raised in town and tank crews were running into the nearby forest, to their vehicles, which had been rolled out of the parks and driven to the assembly area. As soon as I made it to HQ, I opened the sealed packet containing information giving the mustering point for each unit of the division. But my attempts to contact Corps HQ and 5th Army were futile – the lines were down. And so I stepped outside and surveyed the scene: Captain Sharov was organising the loading of our HQ gear onto vehicles, while Colonel Petr Pavlov, the Divisional Commander, stood at the roadside yelling orders to the drivers as they quit town. Meanwhile, German bombers were converging on the fuel depots – our flak gunners opened up, shooting down four planes. Petr Pavlov saw me and called out: 'I'll be at the observation post! We'll be acting on the pre-arranged plan!'

Then he jumped into an armoured vehicle and sped off to the OP, situated north of town at the forest's edge. Already there was a feeling the Germans had arrived – bullets whizzed and shells burst more frequently. Officers' wives, clutching prized possessions in small bundles, hurried past like fugitives on the run. And our HQ column also quit, pulling out of the military station to join Petr Pavlov . . .

A radio-telegram arrived from the 41st Motorized Regiment: 'The Regiment is in action at the border and operationally subordinate to 15th Rifle Corps.' Meanwhile, units of the 87th Rifle Division formed up for a counter-attack as artillerymen heaved their guns into firing positions. 'Shall we strike at Ustilug?' I suggested to Petr Pavlov. 'We can't – remember what General Vladimir Tamruchy said?' – 'To pull out to the muster area . . .' – 'Exactly. Orders are not a joke – especially in war. We can't use our KV-2 heavy tanks – no shells are available. If we strike with T-26s they'll get stuck in the trenches of the Fortified District.' Petr Pavlov remained silent for a second before announcing: 'We'll counter-attack with a battalion of the 82nd Tank Regiment in coordination with the 87th Rifle Division. I'll stay here; you lead the remaining units to the muster area. Send unit commanders to Army and Corps HQs – we need to restore communications.' Then he set a task for Major Alexander Suin, Commander of the 82nd Tank Regiment – kick the Germans out of Vladimir-Volynsky and destroy the depots in case they fell to the enemy.

I led the column to the muster area – enemy aviation circling above, strafing and bombing. We lost a KV-2 tank, which went up in a sheet of flame. Another got bogged down and had to be blown up by its crew.

Lieutenant Talash, who had remained at HQ to destroy documents, arrived, having completed his task. Communications with 5th Army and 22nd Mechanized Corps were still down and the liaison officers I sent had not yet returned. By evening, however, we learned that the Germans had been evicted from Vladimir-Volynsky – at a price. About thirty T-26s had been destroyed by enemy machine-guns, anti-tank rifles and artillery. Major Suin, his face smeared with sweat and blood, showed us a German 'bazooka' anti-tank rifle – too bad our infantrymen had no such weapon. As night fell, officers' wives and children – scared and exhausted – gathered at the command post. We had nothing to give them – not even a blanket. Petr Pavlov ordered their evacuation to Kovel and appointed Sergei Zavorotkin, the Divisional Commissar, to oversee the operation.[7]

The first hours of the war were no less dramatic for the 124th Rifle Division of Filipp Soushy. By 9 a.m. most of its rifle divisions – supported by the 21st Artillery Regiment of the 27th Corps – were engaged in combat with the enemy. Pressurized from the front and with open flanks, Soushy's division was in a perilous state of affairs. The situation deteriorated throughout the day, as the Germans threw Panzers and mechanized units into action. By 11 a.m. the 124th Rifle Division was effectively outflanked, the Germans having almost reached Stoyanov, some 25km from the border. Outnumbered and outclassed in terms of equipment, the Soviet 87th and 124th Rifle Divisions ended the first day of *Barbarossa* like two islands amid a flood of field-grey German soldiery. Mikhail Sandler remembers:

> I found myself, a sergeant, in an automobile company of the 65th Tank Brigade. The brigade was located at Gorodok, 30km from Przemy l and 70km from Lwów.* I was on duty at the Deputy Platoon Commander's position. On the night of Saturday, 21 June, a marvel previously unseen by we Red Army soldiers appeared – beer in kegs. The guys lined up with mess tins, buying half a litre for 20 *kopecks*. Many of us were in our final month before demobilization. We sat in the smoking-room, drank beer, and shared plans for civilian life. The improvized 'bar' stayed open late and we went to bed at 2 a.m. Two hours later, bombs were falling from the sky. Our losses in that first raid were not significant, but it's hard to convey the emotions we felt – it was a shock.

---

* A Polish city for much of its history, Lwów was incorporated into the USSR following the Nazi-Soviet invasion of Poland in 1939.

We knew the war would start sooner or later and had been preparing for it. But when you see your buddy – who'd slept in the neighbouring bunk for two years – killed by bomb splinters, you feel sick at heart. Seems we'd all been issued with 'warrants to proceed to Mogilev Province' . . . [a grim Russian joke – Mogilev is a city whose name derives from the word *mogila* meaning 'grave' – trans.]

At 5 a.m. the Commander of my Automobile Platoon, Lieutenant Frolov, ran up to the barracks, called up five drivers – me included – and told us to load the officers' families onto trucks and take them to Lwów. Engulfed by panic, these wives and children, clutching meagre belongings, boarded the trucks and our column headed off.

We drove down country tracks the whole day, reached Lwów, and stopped in the city centre, near a big church. Someone started shooting at us from the attic of a nearby house. The kids ran to ground, weeping and wailing. We wanted to give them water and dashed into a nearby house to ask for some – no one would help. Instead, they grinned, the meaning of which was clear: 'This is your end, "Soviets".' We hadn't expected this from the 'Westerners' [i.e. former Polish citizens dubbed 'West Ukrainians' after the Soviet invasion of 1939 – trans.]. A couple of days later, we managed to get the officers' families onto a goods train heading east. We couldn't return to Gorodok, as the place had already been captured by the Germans . . .[8]

Chapter 5

'A Hot Day'

While large-scale assaults by German aviation and armour did not occur across the whole of the Białystok Salient, smaller forays were so widespread that not a single sector remained quiet. Sergeant Major Anatoly Loginov of the 87th Frontier Guards Detachment (3rd Frontier Post) recalled that:

> I was on duty in Lobzha, not far from Grodno. Around 2 or 3 a.m. on 22 June heavy bombers flew over at high altitude. The Frontier Post Commander was resting and the *Politruk* was on vacation. According to the regulations, however, a sergeant major was entitled to set operational tasks for border protection, so I assigned a task for the next detail. Suddenly, the sky turned red: 'Well, Sergeant major, is it war or just provocation?' – 'It's war, guys. The Belovsky, Sorokinsky and Malinovsky sectors are all under fire. We're going into action.' The German artillery put down a barrage for about ten minutes, then their infantry advanced while the tanks worked round our flanks. But we were well armed: two large-calibre machine-guns and SVT semi-automatic rifles. I had a PPSh submachine-gun. And we had two good sharpshooters with sniper rifles. In general, border guards are good shots – we were taught to fire in the direction of gunshots and muzzle flashes. A few days earlier we'd virtually been disarmed by the detachment's Head of Technical Supply, who told me to discharge the cartridge belts for the machine-guns. I made a start on this task but stopped as soon as he left. Because of this we could only fight for a couple of hours. But the guys still rose to the counter-attack three or four times. At last the Germans broke through. At 4.30 a.m. a messenger arrived

with orders to quit the border and join regular Red Army units. I sent up a red flare – the signal to withdraw and head for the frontier post. We arrived at the Commandant's office and were formed into units – we'd done our duty.[1]

Private Anatoly Kazakov of the 178th Artillery Regiment (attached to General-Major Sherstyuk's 45th Rifle division), recalls:

The West Ukrainian town of Lyuboml, situated on the River Bug, some 13km from the State Border, was defended by the 45th Rifle Division (whose HQ was located at Kovel). South of the town was a steep rise topped by a topography station – the position of our 178th Artillery Regiment. The regiment was armed with 76mm horse-drawn guns, subordinate to divisional command. Due to inadequate training, severe frosts and an intake of recruits from Azerbaijan and Georgia – who didn't know Russian – our unit was hardly battleworthy. Which brass hat had the bright idea to place such an outfit in the first echelon? Meanwhile, the locals – who had only recently become Soviet citizens – clung to the customs and attitudes of the Polish State. They were mistrustful of the new collective farms and fearful of the NKVD. One local, on examining our clumsy Red Army soldiers, openly declared: 'The Germans will annihilate you . . .'

About 4 a.m. on 22 June shells pounded our position. The first salvo hit the barracks, causing the roof to cave in and the walls to collapse in a cloud of dust and smoke. Then the HQ tents were hit – the battalion commander's arm was shattered, so the chief of staff took over. Now disorder was replaced by sensible action, everyone taking his place according to battle drill. Our horses were pulled from the stables with some difficulty amid the shell-bursts, while the gun crews rolled the guns out of the depots to the relays. Thus the battery cantered to its reserve positions, unknown to the Germans, who continued pulverizing our former location on the hill. Gradually we assembled and counted our losses, which turned out to be light – several soldiers wounded and two horses killed. Later, our field kitchen – forgotten by everyone – turned up and the soldiers stuffed themselves with hot pasta.

A German *rama* [i.e. 'frame', the Russian nickname for the twin-fuselage, twin-engine FW-189 reconnaissance aeroplane – trans.] appeared in the sky but our relays – hidden beneath the awnings of nearby shacks – apparently cheated it, as no shelling followed. Perhaps the aircraft was interested in a more important target . . .

The regiment was largely manned by recruits who had served no more than two months. We felt sorry for these boys, thrown unprepared into the inferno of combat. Again, we were astounded by the short-sightedness or malicious intent of the District HQ. Meanwhile, the sun rose high above the horizon – a hot day was beginning, in both the literal and figurative sense.

An order arrived: the battery must take up fire positions west of Lyuboml, behind the railway. We trotted 2km down country tracks and leaped out at the allocated spot, while the relays rode off to shelter in a nearby grove. We dug in – the shovel is as much a combat weapon as a rifle – I, myself, hacking out a narrow slit trench next to the left wheel of the gun (a soldier's rule is: as soon as you hit the ground, dig a hole for your head – never mind about your arse; then dig deeper; once you're safely hidden, get ready to shoot). We piled parapets around the guns, smoothed and deepened the ramp. Shells were brought by cart and piled behind the guns as a reserve. Signalmen dragged coils of telephone cable to the observation post through a roadside ditch. There was a distance of some 8km between the battery and the OP.

Two hours of quiet followed. The battery was now ready to fight – despite the inhibitory role of the higher HQs (we later heard of some commanders who, having taken casualties, were still ringing HQ for permission to fire – such was the fear of provocation and of taking independent decisions). Then we heard the buzz of aircraft flying from the east – two flights of ground-attack planes were in the air. We were in raptures – our planes were overhead! Imagine our surprise when we spotted black German crosses on the wings. These Messerschmitts were returning to their aerodromes.

About midday a telephone order came from the Battery Commander at the OP: 'Battery! Action! Number One Gun, one shell – fire!' The zeroing-in shell flew off. Then: 'Battery! Two splinter shells – fire!' And finally: 'Battery! Five shells – volley fire!' The guns began to roar, the ground shook, the air thickened with smoke and dust. At which point, Politruk Poleshuk arrived with the news: 'It's not a provocation – the Germans are advancing over the whole front between the Barents Sea and the Black Sea. They've bombed Kiev, Zhitomir, Minsk and other cities. The Party urges us to repulse the enemy!' Our soldiers, inspired, began to chatter: 'We'll reach the Atlantic in three months!'

A German spotter plane appeared. Suddenly, an alien sound mingled with the rumble of our guns – incoming shells were screaming into the battery, scattering soil and splinters, as stinking black smoke engulfed our position. Seeing an explosion between the gun mounts, I dived into my foxhole. Kosharnyi – an assistant gunlayer – also went to ground, clutching a wound in his shoulder. Soveiko – a gun charger – was killed. German shells continued to hammer us while a signalman, yelling from his trench, relayed a message from the Battery Commander: 'Why have you ceased firing? Fire! Volley fire by the whole battery!' Apparently it was not so comfy over at the OP.

How frightful it was to quit my shelter! Taking myself in hand, I manned the gun-sight as a charger crawled up and chambered a shell. The gun-lock clanked. A shot! The recoil knocked me back into the trench. I scrambled out and, through a shroud of dust, saw a terrible scene: shell craters covered our position; a gun had been overturned; shells were scattered all over the place; dead men were lying mangled; wounded men were crawling. And still the Commander kept calling from the OP: 'Lisyak, 0.15 to the right, three shells – fire! Why isn't Gun Number Four firing?'

We kept on firing with three guns. After several hours the barrels were red hot, the paint peeling and bubbling. The oil was overheating in the recoil mechanism and oozing through the screws. The load-limit of the barrels had been exceeded and they were liable to burst. Lieutenant Lisyak – the senior man at the battery – reported to the OP. The Battery Commander reluctantly called the 'All Clear'.

This action was my first – that's why I remember it in detail. The dead guys were picked up – mostly greenhorns – ammo carriers who, lacking entrenching tools, had cowered behind crates. I don't know their surnames.

A strange silence gripped us. For some reason we preferred to talk in whispers . . .

The field kitchen came round and took post in a small ravine. A local guy, Yashka Kramer, was sent over to collect food. A stray German shell exploded near his foot, plastering him in hot pasta, but leaving him otherwise unscathed. Amazing things happen in war!

The Battery Commander telephoned from the OP. Lisyak passed on the message: 'The OP will relocate – limbers to the battery!' We froze in suspense – where are we going? If forward, then our troops were on the advance. If backward, they were on the retreat. The battery formed a marching column and moved onto the road. Lisyak, riding at the head of the column, turned right. But having trotted several hundred metres the column was halted. Lisyak and the gun commanders walked around, examining the terrain. There would be no forward or backward – just a change of firing position . . .[2]

On 22 June the 62nd Rifle Division of Colonel Timoshenko was mainly engaged on its left flank, north of Ustilug. The situation was complicated by the fact the division had gone into combat undermanned: one of its regiments (the 104th) was in reserve in the Podgorodno–Horostkov area, and only two battalions were present in Colonel Petr Gavilevsky's 306th Rifle Regiment, as one battalion had been left on guard duty in Lutsk. Meanwhile, the operations of the 41st Rifle Division (6th Army), deployed south of *Barbarossa*'s main strike, became the first unpleasant surprise for the Germans. These troops, commanded by General-Major Georgi Mikoushev, together with combined border guard units, invaded German-occupied Polish territory to a depth of 3km on an 8km-front. This incursion was explained in the operations logbook of Army Group South in the following way:

> The 262nd I[nfantry] D[ivision] appeared prone to 'the fright of the enemy' and retreated. The eastern wing of the Corps is certainly in [a condition of] crisis. This situation will be rectified by the introduction of the 296th Infantry Division between the battle formations of the 24th and the 262nd Infantry Divisions.[3]

The chief of staff of the 17th Army even requested the transfer of the 13th Panzer Division to assist the 295th and the 24th Divisions.

On the other hand, beside the success of Georgi Mikoushev's division, the 'Achilles heel' of the Soviet 6th Army's position was set up on the first day of the war. The 3rd Cavalry Division was moved forward from the Zolkew area to the Belz–Ugnuw Line, in order to cover the right flank of the Army. According to the Plan of Cover, a cavalry unit – unsuited for manning of static defence sector by virtue of its organizational structure – would have to defend this sector only until the third day of mobilization. It had been contemplated that the 3rd Cavalry Division would then be replaced by the 159th Rifle Division, 'having taken over (the defence sector) from the 3rd Cav[alry] Division after 5 a.m. of the third day of hostilities'. However, no replacement of the cavalry division occurred either on the first day of the war or, indeed, on the third day. And it was that very sector through which the Germans later pushed the 9th Panzer Division. The splitting of Soviet mechanized units began on the very first day of the war. Not knowing the scope of the German advance, the commander of the 6th Army, Ivan Mouzychenko, deployed negligible forces to meet it. In the middle of the day, the 6th Army HQ ordered the commander of the 4th Mechanized Corps to allocate two battalions of medium tanks (32nd Tank Division) and a battalion of motorized infantry to destroy the enemy near Radzehov. The chief of staff of the 63rd Tank Regiment described the events the following way:

> Having turned around, the column headed, as a matter of fact, in the reverse direction. The T-34 I was in, by order of the corps commander, followed Zheglov's machine. For the first

time I was inside a T-34. There'd been no such machines in the reconnaissance battalion I'd been in charge of before my arrival at the regiment. I look closely at the crew, at their conduct, at the way they do their duties. Everything is going well from my point of view. I feel sorry about just one thing: I haven't had a chance to drive this tank or shoot from it. And how badly I need those skills now!

I try to imagine the situation at the State Border. I knew that the 140km sector from Krysynopol to Radymno was covered by two frontier guard detachments, the 41st, 97th, 159th Rifle Divisions, and the 3rd Cavalry Division. They were supposed to be ahead of us. Did they manage to take up their lines on time? What kind of task are they carrying out now? Maybe the regiment's reconnaissance commander, Lieutenant Korzh, who we have sent forward, will be able to clarify something? How badly we need some general information about the enemy . . .

The driver slows down and stops abruptly. 'What's happened?' I shout to the crew commander.

'Air,' he replies.

I open the hatch. The daylight dazzles me for a moment, but at the same moment I notice black puffs of smoke rising far ahead: bomb explosions. The aircraft are getting closer and closer. They are sharp-nosed, with slightly gulled wings. They hang over the column and drop their mortal load one after another. Rumble, whizzing, fire, smoke . . .

Signal flags flash above the commander machine – 'Forward! Follow me!' – as it turns on the spot, crawls over a roadside ditch, and moves towards the forest, gaining speed. Our tank follows. I had time to look around. To our right is the floodplain of the River Shklo. It means we are west of Yavorov. Transport vehicles are blazing on the road, ammo is exploding, several tanks (damaged during the bombing) stand motionless. The German planes turn around unhurriedly and the howling and rumbling begins again . . .

We're already approaching the forest when shells begin bursting right and left of us. The commander's machine jerkily speeds up to evade fire. Our driver also revvs up and soon we find ourselves on the spot of the first tank engagement, which had just been fought by Major Zheglov's battalion. Three German tanks stand stricken on the field, crimson flames rising from their turrets and hatches, dense smoke spiralling, ammo exploding. Our five tanks bog down in the swampy river bed left of the Krakowec road. Three of them keep firing as tankers bustle around, adjusting logs for the tracks to pull themselves out [. . .] A German shell screams over the turret of one of the T–34s. Shots are heard from the other side of the river and explosions are rumbling in our direction . . .

I had lagged behind the regiment's commander at the approach to the River Shklo, and currently I didn't know where he was, or what decision he took when our two battalions came across the enemy. I felt offended that, carrying out the corps commander's order, I found myself in the role of an ordinary tanker, having lost communication with both regimental and divisional HQ. I only knew what I could see for myself, and what I had heard from the company commander, Senior Lieutenant Bestchetnov.

I tried to reach Zheglov's two-way radio. No reply. Fortunately, I managed to contact the second battalion. Having engaged German infantry and tanks they managed to push them back. Kolkhidashvili led the companies forward but, having encountered strong fire from artillery and tanks, he had to stop. Two companies of the first battalion were somewhere on the left flank. I ordered Senior Lieutenant Bestchetnov to establish communications with them. The third battalion, having turned off the road – above which enemy aircraft kept circling – had stopped in the woods nearby and was awaiting orders.

I found regimental HQ at the edge of a grove. An HQ bus stood under pine trees, the radio–station was nearby. The Deputy Chief of staff, Captain Krivosheev, jumped off the bus. His thin, black, eyebrows were scowling: 'The regiment commander has been killed.' A chill crossed my heart. I stared at Krivosheev, unwilling to believe what he had told me. Could it be possible that Zheglov was no more? I took off my helmet, finding no words to express my grief. And Captain Krivosheev, without waiting for my reply, added: 'Kombat [Battalion Commander – trans.] Scheglov is badly wounded.' Then a signalman shouted from the bus:

'Comrade Captain, they want you on the phone!' The divisional commander, Colonel Efim Pushkin, was on the line. Having greeted me dryly he asked:

'How come you didn't safeguard the regiment commander? The first action and such a loss . . .'

'We didn't even know the Germans had broken through the covering units,' I replied after a short pause. 'We thought that infantry was ahead of us . . .'

'You must learn to fight from the very first action,' Efim Pushkin said, adding: 'It's been decided to appoint you as regimental commander. Captain Krivosheev will be the Chief of staff.' Efim Grigorievich Pushkin stood silent for a short while, giving me time to grasp the level of responsibility pinned on me, and then added:

'Lose no time. Take charge of the regiment. This is war. It punishes hesitancy. How do you assess the current situation?'

I reported what I knew. The report obviously dissatisfied Efim Pushkin.

'It's not enough for a competently run outfit,' he pointed out. 'Clarify the situation properly and report back. Get it done before the enemy renews his activity.'[4]

Further south, the situation looked somewhat calmer. Rifle regiments of the 8th Rifle Corps had been ordered to take up defence lines near the border; but the corps commander would not permit the use of artillery before 10 a.m. The 8th Mechanized Corps was roused by alarm at 5.40 a.m. and began moving up to the second echelon of the 26th Army. Hundreds of trucks and tanks moving towards the border were spotted by the Germans and this caused anxiety at 17th Army HQ. The following was recorded in the operations logbook of Army Group South: 'The 17th Army Commander, being impressed by aerial reconnaissance data concerning the march of a large motorized enemy formation from the area of Stryi–Drogobych westwards, initially hesitated to order the advance of the 101st Light Infantry Division.' That was why, in the sector of the 26th Army, the whole day was spent skirmishing along the River San, neither side undertaking large-scale advances. The commander of the 8th Mechanized Corps, Dmitri Ryabyshev, depicted the first day of the war in his memoirs the following way:

> At four in the morning Moscow time, I was awoken by a young Red Army messenger: 'Comrade General,' he addressed to me hurriedly, 'you are wanted on the phone at HQ!' My apartment was not far from HQ, so I quickly made myself ready and several minutes later picked up the phone. The head of the Operations Department of the 26th Army advised that German-Fascist troops had breached our State Border and were engaged in combat against the border guards. Enemy aircraft were bombing our border cities and aerodromes.
>
> 'I ask you not to panic!' he said anxiously, adding, 'We reckon these are provocations. Don't fall for them! Don't open fire at the German aircraft! Await further instructions!'
>
> I decided to make the troops ready for action immediately. I had already arranged to inform my divisional commanders of any outbreak of hostilities via certain code words, known only to us: 'Orderly, summon the divisional commanders to the telephone!' No more than three minutes elapsed and the orderly reported:
>
> 'General-Major Timofei Mishanin and Colonels Ivan Vasiliev and Alexander Gerasimov are on the phone!' I took the receiver and, trying to remain calm, said:
>
> 'Ryabyshev is on the phone.'
>
> 'Timofei Mishanin on the phone,' came the pleasant, gentle voice of the 12th Tank Division Commander, 'listening to you.'
>
> 'Greetings. *Lightning* flashes in the sky.'
>
> 'All clear, Dmitri Ivanovich,' Timofei Mishanin replied hastily. Having wished him luck, I ended the conversation with him. Then the rich bass of the 7th Motorized Division Commander sounded in the receiver:

'Colonel Alexander Gerasimov on the phone.'

'Greetings! How is it at your place? Is the *forest* making noise?'

'It is, but the forester knows his job, Dmitri Ivanovich,' Alexander Gerasimov said in reply.

'See you . . .'. Then the 34th Tank Division Commander, Colonel Ivan Vasiliev, was on the phone. Having greeted him I said:

'*Mountain*, I wish you success!'

'Lightning', 'forest', 'mountain' – these were apparently conventional words, but upon hearing them, the commanders roused their units, and unsealed the packets containing secret directions to move up to the concentration area . . .

Time passed but no instructions came from Army HQ. I stayed by the telephone. Soon a swelling buzz of engines came from the sky: an enemy bomber appeared above the city. The clock hands were showing 4.30 a.m. as the howl of falling bombs burst through an open window, splitting the frames and shaking the floor beneath my feet. The Head of Signals, Colonel Kokorin, came in and reported anxiously: 'Communications with Army HQ are down. There's no cable communication with the Sadovaya Vishnya either. I've sent people to restore my lines. Army communications may be restored only by those who are responsible for it.'

The corps Chief of staff, Colonel Fedor Katkov, wasn't on the spot at the time: he'd left for vacation just before the war. The Acting Chief of staff, Lieutenant-Colonel Tsinchenko, reported that, according to dispatches from our units, the enemy had dropped paratroopers between Drogobych and the Town of Stryi: 'This is . . .', he hesitated to finish the fateful sentence, so I did it for him:

'This is war!'

Losing no time, I ordered a motorcycle battalion, a company of fast BT-7 tanks and a company of motorized infantry to the enemy landing zone. Soon it became apparent that a group of paratroopers had also landed north-east of Drogobych: so I had to allocate forces there too, in order to neutralize the enemy threat. By that time, a dispatch from the commander of the 12th Tank Division, General Timofei Mishanin, arrived, reporting that his units had carried out the order precisely, and on time, and were now at the assigned locations. There were no losses. Soon I received similar dispatches from the other divisional commanders. They had managed to move men and materiel away from the enemy airstrikes and concentrate in the forests. Only one motorized rifle regiment of the 7th Motorized Division, which had been in summer camp, had been caught by the enemy aviation: the battle alarm had sounded too late and, as a result, the regiment suffered heavy losses: seventy men killed and 120 wounded.

I received an order from the 26th Army Commander at 10 a.m. The corps was charged with the task of mustering in woodland 10km west of Sambor by the end of 22 June. This meant we would be placed in reserve. I gave my troops directions straightaway. We came up to the map. The acting chief of staff of the Corps, Tsinchenko, said: 'It may be assumed that all enemy attacks at the border have been repulsed, and our involvement in the operation is not required yet.'

'I think the same,' agreed Lieutenant-Colonel Losev, the head of the reconnaissance department. Looking at the map intently he went on: 'Considering the geometry of the border line, logistical routes, and the approximate strength of enemy troops in our sector, I presume the enemy decided to deal the main blow north of Przemysl. His operations are apparently of a diversion character in other places.'

'And what is your perception of the enemy actions?' I asked Tsinchenko.

'My assumptions are the same.'

I had only assumptions as well. None of us was in a position to assess the current situation, for we didn't know the real scope of the enemy force or what was happening at the border. In the second half of the day, the air groaned with roar of engines and the gnashing of metal. Clouds of smoke rose up into the sky. These were the troops of our 8th Mechanized Corps, heading towards Sambor from Stryi and Drogobych.[5]

The troops of the 12th Army, manning the Carpathian defence lines south of the Lwów Salient, also received orders to unseal their 'red packets' early on 22 June. The 13th and the 17th Corps were to move some 100km across woody, mountainous terrain. The 12th Army's Chief of staff, General B. Aroushnya, remembers:

On 21 June I stayed late at Army HQ (located in Stanislaw), working out the next planned training drill, before eventually returning home. In the fourth hour of the night I was woken by a phone call: 'Comrade General,' the operations orderly reports. 'you are urgently called to the phone by the District Chief of staff, General-Lieutenant Maxim Pourkaev.' I dressed quickly and made off to HQ. The orderly reported: 'The District Commander, General-Colonel Mikhail Kirponos, has just rung up and summoned the Army Commander, General-Major Pavel Ponedelin, and you to HQ. The *Komandarm* [i.e. Army Commander – trans.] hasn't arrived yet.' I reported to the District Commander:

'What's the situation in your sector?' General Mikhail Kirponos asked.

'All is still quiet.'

'Alright. Take a sheet of paper, a pencil, and write down (Kirponos dictated):

At 03.00 today, the German-Fascist aviation bombed Kiev, Odessa, Sevastopol, and other cities. Since 03.30 their artillery has been shelling our frontier posts and Fortified Districts. I order:

1. To rouse the troops by alarm immediately; to disperse them and make ready for action; the aviation to be dispersed to the field airstrips.

2. The units of the Fortified Districts to man the fire emplacements of the FDs.

3. Not to bring the field troops up to the border, so as not to fall for provocations.'

I repeated what I'd written down. 'Carry on,' Mikhail Kirponos said. 'Let the Komandarm ring me up.'

Having hung up, I instructed the orderly to rouse the HQ staff by alarm. Then I began to transmit Kirponos's order via

VCh [secure high-frequency communication lines – trans.] to the corps commanders and Army units. At this time, General Pavel Ponedelin and a Member of the Military Council, Brigade Commissar Ivan Koulikov, arrived. I updated them about the order and the measures undertaken. Soon, the whole HQ staff gathered. Having got familiarized with the situation, the officers set to work.

About an hour later, General Maxim Pourkaev called me up to the 'Bodo' signalling-flag apparatus [used for communication when radio was lacking – trans.] and conveyed the conventional signal for putting the border cover plan into operation: 'KOVO 1941'. I immediately reported this to the Komandarm, in the presence of the Member of the Military Council. We notified the groups and units straightaway.[6]

On the morning of 22 June, troops of the Odessa Military District implemented the border Plan of Cover without serious difficulties. The 35th Rifle Corps moved up to the Lipkani–Ungeni sector, the 2nd Cavalry Corps to the Leovo–Kagul sector and the 14th Rifle Corps (25th, 51st Rifle Divisions) to the Kagul–Izmail–Kilya sector. The reserve troops mustered in the following areas:

- 48th Rifle Corps (74th Rifle Division, the 30th Mountain-Rifle Division) – Bel'tsy, Floresty, Rybnitsa
- 2nd Mechanized Corps (11th, 16th Tank Divisions, 15th Motorized Division) – the Kishinev area
- 18th Mechanized Corps (44th, 47th Tank Divisions, 218th Motorized Division) – Berezino, Tarutino, Ackerman (Belgorod-Dnestrovsky)
- 116th Rifle Division – Nikolaev
- 150th Rifle Division – the Komrat area

Yuly Routman, who found himself in the camp of the 150th Rifle Division (Odessa Military District), remembers:

Back then, I worked as head of Propaganda and Agitation for the Odessa Oblast broadcasting committee. On 21 June I got a phone call at my workplace, summoning me to the Il'ichevky *voencomat* [i.e. district military commissariat – trans.]. The call was from an acquaintance of mine, Lieutenant Kostin – he had issued call-up papers for camp drilling two or three times before. I was hastily preparing a radio program and, having done the job, arrived at the commissariat in the evening. I saw several men by the entrance with bags, which surprised me to a certain extent. Lieutenant Kostin stood by a desk and handed me a call-up paper, advising that, by 9 a.m. on 22 June, I would have to arrive at the 150th Rifle Division HQ, prior to going to camp. When I went home and told my wife what had happened, she was surprised. After all, only recently I had returned from camp, where I'd done service as head of the 6th Department of the Tiraspol FD HQ.

On the morning of 22 June, about 5 a.m., someone tapped on my window. Having opened the door, I saw an unfamiliar lieutenant. Having specified that I was Yuly Routman, he said that I would have to dress and head to the 150th Rifle Division HQ immediately (the HQ was situated in the centre of the city). Upon arrival, I reported to the divisional Chief of staff, Colonel Lyubivyi. The latter ordered me to don uniform immediately. My military rank was Junior Lieutenant. I was appointed as an assistant to the head of the 6th Department of the divisional HQ. The head of it, Lieutenant Kovalenko, handed me a briefcase with documents, and then disappeared somewhere. Thus, I stayed on my own. The division was under the command of General-Major Iosif Khoroun.

At 9 a.m. all staff officers went outside. There was a column of vehicles ready, including the HQ bus and several trucks containing submachine-gunners. Soon my wife arrived. We didn't talk about the outbreak of the war, as we knew nothing about it. Having bid farewell to my wife, I took my place in the bus and soon the column sped off.

Only at noon, when the column stopped and we got off the bus, was a loud-speaker turned on. Viacheslav Molotov's speech was broadcast, declaring that the war had begun, and that Hitlerite Germany, as it was said, had suddenly attacked us. Within twenty-four hours, our 150th Rifle Division, being part of the 9th Army, took up defence lines along the River Prut (Bessarabia).[7]

From 22 June, German troops attempted to capture the crossings over the Prut, attacking Soviet troops in the Sculeni, Ungeni, Felciu areas. But the German Eleventh Army, commanded by Eugen Ritter von Schobert, made no large-scale advance. Instead, it was tasked with keeping the Red Army troops of the Odessa Military District occupied, in order to prevent their transfer to the sector of *Barbarossa*'s main strike. Consequently, the establishment of bridgeheads on the eastern bank of the Prut was von Schobert's principal objective. And the most important of these was situated near the settlement of Sculeni, approximately 20km north of the Romanian City of Iasi. A stubborn defence was planned for it, as described in the operations logbook of the Army Group South:

> At 11.50, at a conference, the Chief of staff of the Eleventh Army raised the question of the necessity to hold, under any circumstances, the Sculeni bridgehead; whose bridge had been destroyed by a Russian air strike, due to enemy pressure building up against the bridgeheads on the River Prut.[8]

The bridgehead near Felciu, which was liquidated by the men of the 2nd Cavalry Corps, led by General-Major Pavel Belov, was of less value. It was cleared in a fierce action between 24–26 June. This operation was conducted under the command of the assistant of the 9th Cavalry Division, Colonel Nikolai Oslikovsky. This action was to be widely covered in Soviet research on the initial period of the Great Patriotic War.

As the Red Army entered the war largely undeployed, most units located in the European part of the USSR didn't engage the enemy on the first day: some learned that war had broken out via radio broadcasts; others when they found themselves at the sharp end of German air strikes; but most divisions passed the first day of *Barbarossa* relatively quietly. Nevertheless, certain divisions had been previously assigned to hold defences at the border. One such outfit was the 24th Rifle Division, whose Commander, Kuz'ma Galitsky, remembered:

It began to grow lighter. As the reader already knows, by that time, Army HQ had completed transmission of the battle alarm order. But our division, as well as some others, which had also lost communications with the Army HQ, knew nothing about it. Suddenly, some time after 04.00 hours, the telephone rang, and I heard the anxious voice of Major Portnov: 'Comrade General, Fascist aircraft are bombing Lida and the aerodromes of the 11th Aviation Division. There are fires in the town and at the aerodrome.' My mind was seared by the alarming thought: the war! Lida was 120–150km from the border, measured from the so-called Suwałki Salient. If it was bombed, it could not be a mere provocation. Yet there was no communication with Army HQ. What should be done? A decision came straightaway: it would be better to be accountable for the unsubstantiated mobilization of the first echelon of troops by alarm than to have done nothing. And so I issued Portnov an order:

'Send a reconnaissance group to Lida in motorcars and a half of the medical unit to assist the wounded. Immediately begin to mobilize the first echelon of the regiment in the camp. Bring materiel and ammo from Volozhin by vehicles, maintain communications with me.'[9]

The Plan of Cover anticipated that Galitsky's division would be transported in vehicles and by railroad:

The commander of the 24th Rifle Division will be provided with the 30th Automobile Regiment, numbering 240 ZIS-5 machines and 625 GAZ-AA machines to transport men, horses and materiel; the commander of the 100th Rifle Division, with the 15th and the 32nd Motorcar Regiments, numbering 269 ZIS-5 machines and 1,140 GAZ-AA machines.[10]

Of course, under the real circumstances of 22 June, any transportation in motor cars was out of the question. Moreover, the unit's original plans were to be altered. Kuz'ma Galitsky continues:

At noon we heard Viacheslav Molotov's speech on the radio. It was the address of the Soviet Government to the people regarding the perfidious attack of Fascist Germany on the USSR. The main thing had become clear: the enemy had unleashed the war against our socialist Motherland, and the Communist Party would rouse the whole people to defend our just cause, to destroy the invading foe [. . .] At 15.00 hours, when the units of the division were already prepared to set off towards Grodno, the restored communications with Minsk began to work at last. And we received a first order, signed by General Vladimir Klimovskikh, conveyed by the assistant of the head of the operations department of the District HQ, Major Petrov:

'The 24th Rifle Division: to head off immediately to the Lida area via Molodechno–Vishnevo–Iv'e–Lida; to be at the disposal of the commander of the 21st Rifle Corps.'

This contradicted a previous order from General Dmitri Pavlov, regarding the move of the division towards Grodno. Because of this, I immediately used the revived line of communications and rang up the head of the operations department of the District, General-Major Ivan Semenov. He confirmed that the move of the division up to the Grodno area was no longer relevant.[11]

The re-targeting of the 24th Rifle Division reflected the plans of the Western Front Command to cover the Druskeniki direction. As the Baltic District Commander had drawn the Supreme Command's attention to the gap on the morning of 22 June, the mustering of forces to fill that gap began in the middle of the day. Galitsky's division was subordinate to the 21st Rifle Corps. At 1.55 p.m. this corps received an order to move up to the Skidel–Ostryna area and prepare a defence line running from Merkine-Druskeninkay Ozery–Skidel–Kovshovo (on the River Neman). By turning the 21st Rifle Corps' front towards the west, the Western Front Command was hoping to prevent a breakthrough of enemy mechanized units from the neighbouring district into the rear of Soviet troops located within the Białystok Salient.

On the first day of the war, most Soviet mechanized corps did not engage the enemy. The mechanized units of the Southwestern Front

– the strongest of all in tank numbers – were no exception, their orders calling for reserve deployment in the second echelon. At this point, it is worth commenting on the Southwestern Front HQ's formal approach to implementing the plan of border cover: a strong mechanized group had been assigned a location of secondary importance from a defence point of view; because of this, Dmitri Ryabyshev's 8th Mechanized Corps would be out of action after the first engagements. A manoeuvre identical to that of the 8th Mechanized was carried out by Andrei Vlasov's 4th Mechanized Corps: only a few of its units had not moved up to the border – the 202nd Motorized Rifle Regiment of the 81st Motorized Division, which had remained in Lwów to carry out garrison duties; and motorized rifle and howitzer regiments of the 32nd Tank Division, which were following their group with a significant delay due to lack of transportation.

On the first day of the war, according to the Plan of Cover, much weaker units moved up to meet the German Panzer wedge: the 9th Mechanized Corps of Konstantin Rokossovsky and the 19th Mechanized Corps of Nikolai Feklenko. Between noon and 2 p.m., both corps struck west from their permanent bases, but they would have to travel several hundred kilometres before engaging the advancing enemy. The 15th Mechanized Corps, subordinate to the HQ of the Southwestern Front, was also moving up to the border according to the Plan of Cover: its 10th Tank Division moved from Zolochev; the 37th Tank Division from Kremenets; and the 212th Motorized Division from the Brody district, to the muster areas located near the demarcation line between the 5th and the 6th Armies. A vanguard party was detached from the 10th Tank Division, consisting of the 3rd Tank Battalion of the 20th Tank Regiment and the 2nd Battalion of the 10th Motorized Rifle Regiment, which, at 9.50 a.m., took off towards Radzehuv with the task of annihilating enemy paratroopers in this area. Soviet troops were unfamiliar with the idea of deep enemy penetrations and often identified German mechanized units (which had pushed deep into the rear) as Airborne detachments. At 10 p.m., having found no Germans in the indicated area, the vanguard of the 10th Tank Division engaged enemy units in the Korchin area (18km closer to the border from Radzehuv), before turning back and switching to the defence of Radzehuv.

At 3 p.m., 6th Army HQ ordered the commander of the 4th Mechanized Corps to detach two battalions of medium tanks from the 32nd Tank Division, and one battalion of motorized infantry from the 81st Motorized Division, to wipe out the enemy in the Radzehuv area. The group was led by Colonel Georgi Lysenko (commander of the 323rd Motorized Rifle Regiment of the 81st Motorized Division). Thus two small but well-equipped detachments of the mechanized units of the Southwestern Front had been sent to the Radzehuv area. They didn't yet know that the 11th Panzer Division, whose crews they were to encounter on the next day, had camped overnight several kilometres to the north.

On 22 June 1941 the German Army successfully capitalized on the advantage of surprise, forestalling a major Soviet mobilization and deployment. The border fortifications – in place for several months at a significant cost in cash – were overcome with comparative ease, as were the modern pillboxes. The capture, intact, of important bridges facilitated the rapid German advance. Meanwhile, on the Soviet side, troops of the Special Military Districts were obliged to engage stronger enemies while on the march to the frontier. And those Soviet divisions that did manage to adopt a defensive posture on the border were simply stretched too thin. Thus, the annihilation of the Soviet near-border armies was a foregone conclusion. Meanwhile, the remainder of the Red Army was facing destruction piecemeal. The German 3rd Panzer Group was wedged between Soviet units in the Baltic region and Belorussia, while local aircraft losses stripped the Soviet Command of reconnaissance assets, rendering it effectively blind. Consequently, the true strength of the 2nd Panzer Group's incursion near Brest went largely unnoticed by the Soviet Command until 24 June. This, coupled with an overestimation of German activity near Grodno, led to a faulty distribution of reserves, which, in turn, precipitated a Soviet collapse by the end of the month.

But it cannot be stated that *Barbarossa* unfolded smoothly in every respect. Guderian's desire to avoid a bloody action at Brest saw him sending tanks north and south of the fortress, over adverse terrain that hampered the speed of advance. Meanwhile, Army Group South met such serious resistance that Hitler diverted his forces south towards Kiev – a decision still surrounded by hot debate.

Finally, it should be stated that, once *Barbarossa* was underway, the Soviet Command *did* seek to neutralize it on 22 June, ordering counter-strikes by mechanized corps. In the Baltic region, these counter-strikes facilitated an orderly retreat to defensive lines along the western Dvina, thus avoiding encirclement. And in the Ukraine, mechanized Soviet counter-attacks slowed the advance of the 1st Panzer Group and, indeed, Army Group South as a whole.

Chapter 6

In the Skies . . .

By the 1930s, technical progress had achieved such a level that aviation had become an independent combat arm, capable of engagement in separate aerial battles. Examples include: the Battle of Britain (summer 1940); the Allied air campaign against the Third Reich (lasting many months); and strikes against German aerodromes shortly before the Battle of Kursk. During these operations, the air forces of contesting sides fought for dominance of the skies or sought to eliminate enemy airfields. The number of enemy aircraft 'kills' became the measure of success. One such aerial battle broke out during the first days of *Barbarossa*.

Although 22 June was, in effect, its 'first act', there is a widespread view that the whole invasion drama was over by lunchtime on that fateful day. Pre-war Soviet plans assumed there would be an aerial battle – fought hundreds of kilometres from the border – occurring in the (hypothetical, as things turned out) 'pocket' of time between the outbreak of hostilities and the mobilization of opposing land forces. Thus, the Plan of Cover of the Western Special Military District envisioned the disruption of German operations 'By successive strikes of combat aviation upon established [enemy] bases and aerodromes'; while Soviet aerial combat operations would 'annihilate the enemy Air Force and establish air supremacy from the first days of war'.

Before the war, Soviet aviation specialists had been tentatively assessing the possibility of destroying German air assets *in situ*. A statement by General-Lieutenant Pavel Rychagov of the Red Army Air Force, made at a conference for commanding officers in December 1940, illustrates the sense of caution:

Mastery of the air during a front operation will be achieved by:

1. Annihilation of the enemy Air Force on aerodromes, with simultaneous strikes upon its rear installations (front-line bases, maintenance bodies, fuel depots, ammunition depots).
2. Annihilation of the enemy Air Force in the air and over the battlefield.
3. The achievement of numerical superiority.
     The first task is the most complicated to implement as [. . .] it is necessary to catch the enemy's aviation unawares [while stationed] on his aerodromes [. . .] [this] represents a significant difficulty under the current depth of deployment, and the ability of aviation to relocate from one aerodrome to another. Most of these raids will fail.[1]

Thus Pavel Rychagov did not exclude strikes on enemy aerodromes, but saw such a strategy as 'complicated' and probably fruitless. His view was supported by Evgeni Ptoukhin, the Air Force Commander of the Kiev Special Military District:

The first operation, most difficult, most problematical, is to win air supremacy and to annihilate the materiel of the enemy air force on his aerodromes and in the air. The most difficult and complex operation![2]

At the same conference, General Grigory Kravchenko – the Air Force Commander of the Baltic Special Military District – expressed the following assessment, based on personal experience:

Aerial combat is the main thing. I don't believe the information in the press, telling of heavy aircraft losses on aerodromes. Surely, it is not right. It is not true when they write that the French lost up to 1,000 planes on aerodromes. I base this on my own experience. During the action at Khalkhin-Gol [Soviet–Japanese conflict in Mongolia in 1939 – trans.] I had to make several sorties to destroy just one aerodrome. I would take off with fifty to sixty planes, but there were only eighteen [enemy] planes at this aerodrome! And so I reckon that the numbers given by the press about losses on aerodromes are incorrect.[3]

Grigory Kravchenko was not alone in this opinion; even before Pavel Rychagov's speech, the Commander of the Far East Front, Grigory Shtern, stated: 'It is worth noting that, after all, air supremacy is won not by strikes on aerodromes. It is won by the destruction and neutralization of the enemy in the air.' But the words of Grigory Kravchenko and Grigory Shtern should not be considered the official – or even the prevailing – opinion of Soviet Air Force commanders. In his concluding remarks, Pavel Rychagov resolutely stated:

> Comrades Kravchenko and Shtern, who have spoken here, are inclined to believe that the main destruction of the enemy will be carried out in the air, not on the ground. I have always been an opponent of these extremities. We must be capable of battering the enemy both on the ground and in the air.[4]

To spite the opponents, Pavel Rychagov cited the successful destruction of Japanese aircraft on the aerodrome at Nanking. Pavel Rychagov also argued that a poorly trained pilot may be shot down during his first dogfight (i.e. it is impossible to use him efficiently to fight the enemy in the air) but could successfully destroy enemy aircraft on an aerodrome during a ground attack. Generally speaking, the assessment made by Soviet military specialists may be evaluated as cautious and balanced, without extremities. Nevertheless, Pavel Rychagov was right to view the task of annihilating enemy air assets on the ground as overly ambitious and requiring meticulous preparation. After all, German aerial reconnaissance – which played a key role in *Barbarossa*'s early successes – had been conducted over a lengthy period before the war even began.

These flights (conducted by the so-called 'Kommando Rowehl', named after Colonel Theo Rowehl) initially used civilian airliners for reconnaissance and had been scouting Soviet airspace since the mid-1930s. The Soviet Government was aware of this, making several ineffective protests via diplomatic channels. Rowehl's reconnaissance activities even continued after Hitler's ban on scouting flights over Soviet territory from September to December 1940 (for fear that an untimely intensification of aerial activity might spook the enemy). Consequently, one shouldn't think that Soviet leaders had lapsed into idiocy in 1941: the fact is, the antics of German reconnaissance planes had simply become customary.

Rowehl's team resumed its work over the USSR during the first months of 1941: one squadron flew from Kraków aerodrome in Poland, one from Bucharest in Romania and one from the Hamina aerodrome in Finland. Contrary to widespread opinion, Rowehl's group was not equipped with high–altitude aircraft until 1941; before that date the group flew Do-215s, Ju-88s, He-111s and even Me-110s. Soviet fighter-pilot, Vitali Klimenko, remembers:

> The German boundary was 100–125km from Siauliai. We could sense its proximity on our very skin. First, manoeuvres of the Baltic Military District were conducted continuously; second, an aviation squadron was on watch (in full combat readiness) at the aerodrome – or at least a flight of fighters. We frequently came across German aerial scouts but had no orders to shoot them down, so we merely saw them off to the border. What was the point of sending us into the air – to say hello or what?![5]

One of Rowehl's first high–altitude flights, conducted on 6 January 1941, illustrates the characteristic pattern of German aerial scouting. A plane crossed the border, flew 24km beyond it, then circled 161km over Soviet territory before returning home. Of course, only high-altitude planes flew deep into Soviet territory and, since the USSR lacked full radar vision in 1941, flying above 10,000m was relatively safe.

But not all reconnaissance flights went smoothly. On 15 April 1941, a high-altitude Ju-86R with civilian markings, which had taken off from Kraków to photograph the Zhitomir area, was forced to lose height due to engine problems. The plane was shot down by a Soviet fighter near Rovno. After crash-landing, the pilots (Uffz. Flugzeugführer Schnetz and Uffz. Beobachter Walther) were arrested by the NKVD. The German fliers managed to spoil the reel of film containing their reconnaissance photos, but failed to hide a topographical map of the USSR's border area, which was sufficient evidence against them. During interrogation, the Germans claimed they had simply gone astray during a blind-flying exercise. According to the German version of subsequent events, both airmen were soon liberated by advancing German troops and returned to 'Kommando Rowehl'. Generally speaking, however, it was not easy to shoot down a Ju-86R flying at high altitude.

A dramatic accident that entailed the loss of two modern MiG-3 fighters occurred in the Baltic area on 10 April 1941. On that day, an attempt was made to intercept an unrecognised plane, which had invaded Soviet airspace at high altitude. A flight of three Soviet fighters from the 31st Fighter Aviation Regiment (FAR) of the 8th Integrated Aviation Division (IAD) took off from one of the Kaunas aerodromes. Only one of them, flown by Junior Lieutenant Akimov, made it home. One pilot, Aksyutin, landed by parachute, but Junior Lieutenant Evtushenko crashed with his plane. All three MiGs had fallen into a spin due to jerky manoeuvring at high altitude and low speed: only Akimov managed to pull out. Apparently, unfamiliarity with the new MiG machine was to blame – Evtushenko had never flown a MiG-3 before and had only made thirteen flights in a MiG-1, without ascending higher than 5,000m.

From mid-April to mid-June 1941, the Rowehl Group systematically flew three flights a day. The main task was to update information collected during analogous flights in the spring of 1940. On 21 June 1941, Rowehl's 4th Squadron returned to its home base at the Berlin–Rangsdorf aerodrome, in order to perform reconnaissance work in the West. The remaining three squadrons continued their activities over the USSR after the onset of *Barbarossa*. The meticulous work of the Rowehl Group enabled German planners to prepare a gigantic operation, designed to destroy Soviet air assets in the border districts on the ground.

The Baltic Military District was not a high priority in Soviet military plans and air units lacked new equipment. The SB bombers and I-153 fighters were the most typical aircraft of the District (only the 15th and 31st Fighter Aviation Regiments, which had been equipped with the modern MiG-1 and MiG-3, were untypical – and it is worth noting that provision of the 'first series' MiGs exposed the airmen of these regiments to all the 'teething problems' associated with new aircraft). On the eve of *Barbarossa* the Baltic Special Military District's air assets consisted of five fighter aviation divisions (IADs): the 4th IAD, commanded by *Kombrig* (Brigade Commander – trans.) Sokolov (195 airworthy aircraft); the 6th IAD, commanded by Colonel Ivan Fedorov (208 airworthy aircraft); the 7th IAD, commanded by Pavel Petrov (199 airworthy aircraft); the 8th IAD, commanded by Colonel Vasili Goushin (150 airworthy aircraft); and the 57th IAD, commanded by Colonel Kuz'ma Katichev (242 airworthy aircraft) – a total of 994 airworthy aircraft. Meanwhile, the demarcation between Army Group North and Army Group Centre, which ran through the Baltic Special Military District, meant that local Soviet airmen faced the combined force of VIII Air Corps (from Air Fleet 2, attached to Army Group Centre) and I Air Corps (from Air Fleet 1, attached to Army Group North) – a total of some 1,468 combat aircraft. Another serious weakness in the Baltic Special Military District's air defences was the state of the aerodrome network. A report concerning the Northwestern Front's air operations, written in the summer of 1942, characterized the dispersal of aircraft across the District as follows: 'At the beginning of hostilities, the Air Force of the Baltic Special Military District had up to seventy aerodromes, of which twenty-one were permanent [and] forty-nine operational . . .'

The first strike on the Baltic District's aerodromes occurred before *Barbarossa*'s opening artillery barrage. Heavy Bf-110 fighters crossed the border at 2.50 a.m. on 22 June and, 5 minutes later, dropped bombs on Alytus aerodrome. This attack had no substantial effect: only a handful of fighters belonging to the 15th and the 31st Regiments of the 8th IAD were based at the aerodrome. The most powerful strike fell on the 8th IAD's Kaunas aerodrome – most Soviet aircraft were destroyed on the ground (still parked in rows), while those few that did take off were hit before gaining altitude. Meanwhile, an aerodrome near Libava (Liepaja) was blasted in a 'turkey-shoot'. Oberleutnant M. von Kossart, of Battle Wing (KG1) 'Hindenburg', recalled that, during the first attack on Libava, German dive-bombers pounced on uncamouflaged planes, parked as if on parade. Ostensibly, only one anti-aircraft machine-gun (stationed near the airstrip) returned fire but did no damage.

According to von Kossart, the German two-way operators intercepted a Soviet transmission in plain text: 'There is no air cover. Our fighter regiment has been annihilated by bombs.'[6] The aerodrome suffered two further attacks, as described by von Kossart:

> Although a large number of fighter planes were parked on the field, neither the first nor the third raid encountered resistance. While the first strike had been fairly swift, the third deliberately destroyed the airstrip and damaged the [remaining] planes. During the second attack, the [Soviet] I-16s were readied for action only at the approach of [our] bombers. The Russians took off and engaged in combat, but no order was discernible in their actions [. . .] Each [pilot] attacked by himself, shooting from about 500m before going straight into a dive . . .[7]

A Soviet pilot of the 10th Fighter Regiment, Vitali Klimenko, remembers:

> We found [female] acquaintances and went with them to the House of Culture [i.e. a social club – trans.] of the Siauliai military garrison, where we sang, watched movies or danced. We were young, after all, just twenty years of age! My girlfriend was a beautiful Lithuanian girl, a hairdresser, named Valeria Bunita. On Saturday, 21 June 1941, I saw her and arranged to go to Lake Rikevoz [probably Lake Rykeva, located near Siauliai – trans.] to take a stroll on Sunday. At that time we lived under canvas in a summer camp near the aerodrome, the manoeuvres of the Baltic Military District being ongoing just then. I awoke about five, thought that it would be good to get up earlier to have time for breakfast, then to go to Valeria's place and head off to the lake.
>
> I heard planes buzzing. The third squadron was on watch at the aerodrome; they flew I-15s, nicknamed 'coffins' due to accidents that had been occurring with them time and again. Here we go, I thought, it's a raid from Panevezys [obviously the pilot mistook the German attack for the local military manoeuvres – trans.], and these guys have missed it. I tossed aside a tent flap and saw planes with German 'crosses' strafing

the tents. I shout: 'Guys, it's war! Watch out – it's a raid!' Everyone leaped out and saw that there were killed and wounded in the neighbouring tents. I pulled on my overall, grabbed my map-case, and ran towards the hangar. I told a technician: 'Come on, roll the plane out!' The planes on watch, which had been lined up nicely, were already ablaze. I turned the engine on and took off. I made circles around the aerodrome as I didn't know where to fly or what to do! Suddenly, another I-16 joined me, dipping its wings: 'Attention! Follow me!' I recognized Sashka Bokach, commander of a sister flight. Off we flew towards the border.

The border's breached – we see columns on the march, villages on fire. Sashka dived into the attack and I followed him. We made two approaches. The enemy columns were so dense it was impossible to miss. But for some reason they were placid and their flak guns didn't shoot. I was afraid of losing my leader – it would be easy to go astray! We landed on the aerodrome, taxied into a caponnières. A vehicle appeared from the command post: 'Was it you who made the flight?' – 'It was.' – 'Off to the command post!' We went to the CP. The Regimental Commander says: 'Arrest them. Put them in the guardroom. Ban them from flying. Who let you attack? Do you know what's what? I don't know either! It may be some kind of provocation, but you shoot! What if they were our troops?' I thought: 'Two cubes off my collar [i.e. officer's rank insignia – trans.], I'm gonna be demoted! I'd just been home on leave as a lieutenant and all the girls were mine – and now I'm gonna be a private! How will I show my face at home?!' But when, at 12 o'clock, Viacheslav Molotov made his speech, we were transformed from villains into heroes. But we were having a hard time! Losses were heavy – many planes destroyed and the hangars burned out. Only two of us out of the whole regiment put up some resistance without waiting for orders.

I remember that, after midday, some squadron commander (who had had a chance to master it) took off in the only MiG-1 present in the regiment. At that moment, a German reconnaissance plane came over: the squadron commander converged on it but wasn't shooting. I thought: 'What are you doing?!' He peeled off, converged once more, but again there was no fire. When he landed we went to clarify the problem. He said: 'The trigger doesn't work.' But it was blocked by the safety frame! He should have just flipped it back!

By the end of the day, about twelve operable planes remained on the aerodrome, and experienced pilots flew them over to Riga via the Mitava aerodrome. The regiment's personnel retreated in trucks, refuellers and maintenance vehicles – whatever could move . . .[8]

The situation was depicted the following way in the above-mentioned report on the operations of the Air Force of the Northwestern Front:

On the second day of the war the situation required the relocation of fighter aviation regiments to aerodromes of the second and the third zones of the Mitava–Dvinsk line. The aerodrome network of the Baltic Special Military District was poorly developed [. . .] The second and the third zones had not been extended, and for this reason the relocation was extremely difficult.[9]

Under these conditions heavy losses were predictable. According to the operations report of the Northwestern Front, dispatched to the Chief of Staff of the Red Army on 22 June at 22.00 hours, the Front's air losses were fifty-six aircraft destroyed and thirty-two damaged on the aerodromes. But recent research suggests the Baltic District lost ninety-eight aircraft: some sixty planes considered destroyed, the rest seriously damaged.

The organization of the Western Special District's air assets was typical for that time: there were integrated aviation divisions of mixed composition subordinate to the armies HQ, and several specialized aviation divisions subordinate to the Front HQ. Accordingly, the 11th Integrated Aviation Division, commanded by Colonel Petr Ganichev, was subordinate to the 3rd Army; the 9th IAD, commanded by Hero of the Soviet Union General-Major Sergei Chernykh, to the 10th Army; the 10th IAD, commanded by Colonel Nikolai Belov, to the 4th Army. The army aviation divisions were meant to provide their assigned land units with direct support. The specifics of these tasks had determined the stationing of air divisions close to the border, in the immediate vicinity of the army HQs they were meant to support.

The subordination of Red Air force units to the Army was introduced in 1940, following the Soviet-Finnish 'Winter War', which highlighted poor coordination between aviation and ground units. But in June 1941, this scheme prevented Air Force commanders from massing aviation at the critical points of the German advance. The situation was worsened by a cumbersome battle control system, totally unsuited to fluid combat situations, with the upshot that aviation units frequently arrived too late to be of use. And in 1941, on the eve of *Barbarossa* aviation regiments were supplied with new aircraft: consequently, when the Germans attacked, there were two complements of planes on many aerodromes, both old and new. The Tarnovo aerodrome of the 9th IAD provides a good example of the problems mentioned above: it was only 12km from the border; it had no hangars, no caponnières, and no specially kitted airstrip; and crammed onto its 1,400m x 1,100m field were over 100 planes, around half of which were modern MiGs. The Tarnovo aerodrome may have been an extreme case – it was closer to the border than the rest and jam-packed with planes – but other airfields were also vulnerable. For example, seventy ground-attack I-15bis and I-153 planes were based at the Malye Zvidy aerodrome, a mere 20km from the border.

Fig. 5: Table showing deployment of aviation regiments belonging to the 9th IAD.

AERODROME	REGIMENT	DISTANCE TO BORDER	AIRCRAFT (QTY)	TOTAL
Tarnovo	129th FAR	12km	MiG-3 (57) + I-153 (52)	109
Doloubovo	126th FAR	22km	MiG-3 (50) + I-16 (23)	73
Sebourchin	41st FAR	50km	MiG-3 (56) + I-153 (52)	108
Vysoko-Mazovetsk	124th FAR	40km	MiG-3 (70) + I-16 (29)	99
Borisivshina	13th FBR	70km	Ar-2 (22) + SB (29)	51

'Having reviewed the composition of the 9th IAD, the reader might reasonably ask: 'Where were the masses of obsolete planes the

Red Army Air Force was so famous for in 1941?' Of course, not all FARs of the Western Special Military District had two complements of aircraft at their aerodromes. The 11th Division had two fighter regiments equipped with I-15bis, I-153, I-16 and one bomber regiment, which was in the process of replacing SBs with Pe-2s. The 10th IAD consisted of two FARs (equipped with I-16s and I-153s), one ground-attack regiment and one bomber regiment. The latter had received ten Il-2s and ten Pe-2s, but familiarization with the new equipment had barely begun. Consequently, pilots had to go into action in obsolete planes. To some extent the deficiencies of equipment were compensated by the skills of crews: judging from the results of pre-war manoeuvres and check-ups, the 10th IAD was considered the most battleworthy in the District.

The so-called 'Front Group' was at the disposal of the Western Special Military District Command and consisted of: the 43rd Fighter Aviation Division, the 12th and 13th Bomber Aviation Division, the 3rd Aviation Corps of Long-Range Bombers (the 42nd and the 52nd Aviation Divisions) and two new aviation divisions being raised (the 59th Fighter and the 52nd Integrated). The 'Front Group' was stationed east of Minsk, and the long-range bomber divisions in the Smolensk area. One shouldn't think that, in the Western Military District, the Soviet Air Force had abandoned the practice of placing aircraft at the disposal of land-army commanders. It had been contemplated that, once war broke out, the 59th and the 60th Aviation Divisions, along with the 43rd Division, would be attached to the 13th Army. The Western Military District had 1,789 aircraft in total, not including training, signals and spotter machines.

Air Fleet 2, commanded by Albert Kesselring, was ranged against the Air Force of the Western Special Military District. Kesselring's force was subdivided into two 'Air Corps' – II and VIII. The II Air Corps (commanded by General B. Loerzer) was tasked with supporting the German Fourth Army and 2nd Panzer Group; the VIII Air Corps (commanded by General W. von Richthofen) was to support the Ninth Army and 3rd Panzer Group. Air Fleet 2 had a total of around 1,600 machines, including reconnaissance and transport aircraft plus planes allocated to interact with land units. Considering that only the VIII Air Corps operated in the Baltic

Special Military District during the first days of *Barbarossa*, it might appear that the Soviet Air Force held the numerical advantage: but it must be noted that the incursion of the German Army Group Centre into the Baltic sector tipped the balance in favour of the invaders.

German aircraft (crewed by pilots experienced in night flying) crossed the Soviet border at high altitude during the night of 21/22 June, prior to *Barbarossa*'s opening artillery barrage. The Soviet airmen who fought in the 129th Regiment remembered the first morning of the war like this:

The siren screamed: 'Battle alarm! Battle alarm!' Fastening broad belts with heavy TT pistols in leather holsters, buttoning up blouse collars, the officer-airmen and technicians of the 129th FAR bolted out of the tents [. . .] Mechanics and gunsmiths grabbed rifles with fixed bayonets, leather ammo pouches, gas masks. Drivers of the aerodrome services battalion started up the engines of special machines: fuel trucks, starter-vehicles with long 'trunks', open trucks with containers of compressed air, all hurried up to the aerodrome. Every vehicle had its own assignment. All were necessary; without them it's impossible to make any plane operation-ready [. . .] Soon the engines of MiG-3s and 'Chaikas' [Russian for 'gull', a common nickname for the I-153 – trans.] shuddered into life.

Only two men remained outwardly quiet. They were the regimental commissar and the recently appointed regimental commander, Yuri Berkal: both understood the seriousness of the situation better than anyone. The time had come to show what the young fighter pilots were capable of. Yuri Berkal scrutinized them: there were no signs of bewilderment or fear on their faces. Each knew his place, his job, and that was pleasing. Holding his anxiety in check, the regimental commander – coolly as if setting up a regular task for a training flight – said: 'Three squadrons to provide cover for the towns of Ostrów-Mazowieckie, Zambrów and Łomzha, and the fourth – for our aerodrome.' It was no secret that these towns were near the border. Beyond them was Poland and Germany . . .

The aerodrome began to buzz like a beehive. The observation flight of three planes took off. Yuri Berkal looked at his watch – 4.05 a.m. A white flag waved and the first squadron, then the second, the third and the fourth were in the air. Two groups of MiG-3s headed towards Ostrów-Mazowieckie and Zambrów, nine 'Chaikas' towards Łomzha, the other nine remained to cover the aerodrome.[10]

Already, 3 squadrons (12 MiG-3s and 18 I-153s) of the 129th FAR were aloft. Twelve Me-109s, which converged upon the aerodrome, failed to succeed and one of them was even considered shot down. The next raid of eighteen He-111s was also successfully repulsed. Three downed German planes were claimed after the dogfight. Pilots Anatoly Sokolov, Alexander Kouznetsov and Venidikt Nikolaev bagged one He-111 each. German sources don't confirm the loss of these planes. Having run out of fuel, the Soviet fighters closed in for landing under cover of the fourth (reserve) squadron. Nevertheless, the 'conveyer belt' of air raids would not stop, and could not be held in check. By 10 a.m., 27 MiG-3s, 11 I-153s and 6 training machines had burned out as a result of bomb raids and ground attacks on Tarnovo aerodrome. Bomb explosions had made the airfield unusable for take-offs and landings so the 129th FAR's commander decided to relocate. Vsevolod Olimpiev, commander of the Telephone Section of the Signals Company, 9th IAD HQ, remembers:

On 21 June 1941 I was already snoozing with the Sunday leave warrant in my pocket, when I heard the orderly bark: 'Take up your arms!' I glanced at my watch – it was about 2 a.m. The company quickly lined up in the HQ backyard. The battle alarm hadn't surprised us, for a regular drill had been anticipated. Uncommon orders – setting up an aerial observation post on the tower of the HQ building, getting battle ammo and hand grenades, loading the reserve stock of cable in a car – were perceived as simulating real combat conditions. I was young and inexperienced, and did not suspect the worst.

My section began its customary work in the darkness of a moonless night, wiring a field telephone to a reserve command post, located at a farmstead several kilometres away from town. It was almost fully light when our special truck – designed to unwind cable – reached a military aerodrome on the outskirts of town. All was quiet. Our attention was caught by 37mm guns hidden in caponnières along the airfield, guarded by crews with helmets and armed with carbines. Such semi-automatic flak guns were a novelty back then. Our vehicle was no more than half a kilometre away from the aerodrome when we heard explosions and machine-gun bursts. Having looked back, we saw planes diving on the aerodrome, glittering tracers of shells and bullets, bomb blasts. The terrible reality became clear to us when black crosses became visible on a bomber pulling out of a dive above us.

The first half of 22 June I was on duty by the telephone at the command post of the commander of the 9th IAD, Hero of the Soviet Union, General-Major Chernykh. Telephone communications with aviation regiments stationed in different towns of the Białystok Oblast, and on field aerodromes along the border, had been interrupted [. . .] Communications with some regiments were established via radio. As judged from Chernykh's gloomy face, the news was bad. Gradually, the terrifying reality was emerging: most of our planes had been destroyed on the ground by bombing raids or strafing from the air – even by artillery fire. Nevertheless, aerial combat was conducted all day long above Białystok by flights on duty, and all those who had managed to take off . . .

I spent the second half of this tragic day in a roadside ditch just outside town. A big armoured unit sped past, heading west, and tearing our telephone cable in several places. With great difficulty I managed to restore communications with divisional HQ, which possibly saved my life. At the end of the day I received a telephone order to leave everything behind and get back to HQ as soon as possible. Two dramatic pieces of news awaited me there. All aviation units had been ordered to quit town immediately and retreat eastward. Such a decision was definitely justified, not only by huge losses of aircraft, but also by the rapid advance of German tank units trying to encircle Białystok from north and south. The second news was no less overwhelming: the Air Force Commander of the Baltic Special Military District, General Ivan Kopets, had shot himself. I used to come across him at divisional HQ – a tall, young, general in leather overcoat remained in my memory. Apparently, he was one of those who had understood his responsibility for the destruction of the District Air Force, which was to tell fatefully upon our military failures of the summer and autumn of 1941.

Late in the evening of 22 June, a long column left Białystok and was far beyond the city by early Monday morning. Only servicemen with blue collar badges were in the vehicles – pilots without planes, aviation technicians, signallers, commissaries. Thus my long wartime journey began . . .[11]

Another factor that significantly complicated Soviet airmen's lives was the mastering of new equipment, which was not achieved without 'teething troubles', even in combat situations. Problems with equipment appeared in the 124th FAR of the 9th IAD before war broke out. In early June, during a training flight, one of the regiment's MiGs shot off a propeller vane due to a malfunction of the synchronizer. On the morning of 22 June, Captain Krouglov and Junior Lieutenant Dmitri Kokorev took off into the air: when German twin-engine planes appeared over the aerodrome, the Soviet pilots attacked; but Kokorev's guns failed after the first shots. Dmitri Kokorev kept his cool, however, and rammed the enemy, chopping off part of the empennage of a Bf-110 from II/SKG-210. Debris from the German plane fell north-east of Vysoky-Mazovetsk, and Kokorev's damaged MiG-3 landed in a field nearby. This Messerschmitt was the first German-confirmed 'kill' by Soviet pilots. But the repulse of this first strike was only the beginning of the air battle. Later, the Germans attacked the 124th FAR's aerodrome with alternating strikes by Bf-110s and He-111s: the Soviet regiment lost thirty machines.

Meanwhile, it was a similar story for other regiments of the 9th Aviation Division: Soviet planes, having withstood the first strike, became victims of successive raids. In total, the division lost 347 planes out of 409. It happened because the Divisional Commander,

Sergei Chernykh, lost his head and failed to move machines and equipment away from enemy strikes. Later, General Chernykh would be accused of criminal inaction, arrested, court-martialled and executed.

Two groups of twin-engine Bf-110s had been charged with the destruction of Soviet planes on the aerodromes of the Białystok Salient. The logbook of Group I, of the Fast Bomber Wing SKG210, vividly depicts the situation of the first day of the war:

> A hundred sorties have been made today. After a regular sortie, Major W. Storp (the Group Commander) created a stink, as his orders on concentration were no longer heeded and airmen were conducting their own war. Some crews have made six sorties each this day. In total, the Geschwader has made thirteen air-raids on fourteen aerodromes, destroyed 344 planes on the ground, and shot down eight planes in the air.[12]

The proximity of the border was the reason aviation units were readied for action on the initiative of junior commanders, and not only in the 9th Aviation Division. At about 3 a.m., the Commander of the 11th IAD, Petr Ganichev, received alarming information from the HQ of the 122nd FAR – the rumble of tank engines had been clearly heard near its aerodrome. Ganichev raised the alarm and flew off towards Grodno in an I-16, so as to familiarize himself with the situation. As a result of this timely alarm, the 122nd Regiment managed to get aloft fifty-three I-16s prior to the arrival of German bombers. Only fifteen (mostly inoperative) planes remained on the ground to become victims of German strikes. However, no destruction occurred during the first enemy raid; but, their turn, the pilots of the 122nd Regiment claimed four enemy 'kills', recognized as Do-17s. The commander of a flight from the 122nd FAR, Sergei Dolgoushin, recalled:

> The regiment had recently relocated from Lida to the Novi Dvor aerodrome in Belorussia, situated 5km from the border. On Friday [20 June 1941 – ed.] morning, me and Serezha Makarov reconnoitred the Suwałki aerodrome. It was crammed with aircraft! On the same day, I reported the results of the reconnaissance to Dmitri Pavlov, Ivan Kopets and

Commander Petr Ganichev, who had flown down. I reported and went to the parking lot, where we were preparing for a sortie, refuelling planes. Suddenly I saw a vehicle approaching and General-Lieutenant Ivan Kopets jumps out. I got agitated and he said: 'What's your name? Will you give me your plane for a flight? Don't worry, Sergei, I won't break it!' Then he said: 'How's the plane?' – 'It's good, the engine works well. Nothing special about it, an ordinary I-16, but with cannons. During landing, keep the speed about 5km higher.' I gave him my map-case, rubber bands to keep it on the lap, and a piece of paper. They took off: Ivan Kopets, Petr Ganichev and the Regimental Commander, Colonel Alexander Nikolaev. Soon they returned and taxied over. I came up and Ivan Kopets got out: 'The plane is good indeed. Everything you said proved correct. But we were unable to count them [the aircraft at Suwałki – ed.] with much accuracy, and I didn't want to hang around there for too long.' They flew away and a commission from the Air Force arrived at the spot, headed by a Deputy Head of the Operations Department, a colonel.

On Saturday [evening], 21 June, [after] we'd done our flying, we were told: 'Remove weapons and ammo boxes, and stow them separately.' That was stupid [. . .] I said to the pilots of my flight: 'Let's leave the ammo in! Everything will be alright.' Me and my mate went to the Novi Afon station and bought a couple of vodka bottles and sprats – maybe we would go fishing on Sunday and have a drink next evening. On Saturday we had a sip before dinner, but there was still vodka and sprats for the Sunday.

At 2.30 a.m. [22 June – ed.] we heard the alarm signal. The small case is always ready – the one you take with you. There are trunks, singlet, tooth powder, tooth brush, shoe brush, clothes-brush, the razor too – and that was it. We ran to the planes with these cases. We ran up to the planes and took the covers off. Technicians began to try the engines, warming them up. It was time to carry cannons and machine-guns. Since we hadn't taken off the ammo boxes, my flight – all three planes – was the first to get ready. I went and reported to the Squadron Commander that the flight was ready. He didn't ask me how we'd managed to get ready before the rest . . .

The day was breaking (I forgot, on Saturday they had sent us a Pe-2 to remind us what it looked like, so we could tell its silhouette from that of the Bf-110) [. . .] and at that moment two planes approached the aerodrome from the south – apparently 'Pe-2s'. Suddenly, a long burst shot from one of them towards the parking lots. All was clear: we'd been strafed by a '110'. We found out on the phone that there were casualties – it had definitely been a German and he had shot at us. We spread our planes and prepared them. Then we saw six planes coming. What was that? Drilling or what? Again, we didn't understand anything. We decided they were MiG-3s from Białystok. But they turned around and began to pounce on us – first with machine-guns, then with bombs. We ran from the planes, tried to hide in slit-trenches, but they were full of soldiers! We saw a shack and rushed towards it. The Germans noticed us running and shot a burst at this shack. The shack had a thatched roof – it caught fire and they left. We had no considerable losses: one machine was smashed. Serezha Makarov couldn't start the engine, but I began to run off. The engine was cold and wouldn't run on full power, so to warm it up I let it run say 500m before returning to the starting point. Suddenly a '109' came over – just one machine. He began shooting at me as if I were a quail! I need time to take off then retract the 'legs' [i.e. undercarriage – trans.]. In order to do so I have to turn a hand-winch forty-three times! So, I am flying just above the ground, being strafed. When I folded the 'legs', my right hand became free: I was capable of manoeuvring. Finally, he left me. I was gradually gaining altitude and when he was approaching I shot at him. He had little chance to shoot me down – just a waste of time.

I flew towards Grodno, had a look at what was happening down there. Our border troops were retreating across the Néman. I flew along the border. There was a German spotter plane. I converged on him, smacked from all guns and downed him straightaway! I landed and reported: 'They've crossed the border, moving towards us.' I pointed on the map: 'The infantry here, the tanks down here.' No sign of our troops. We had just begun to refuel when the Squadron Commander came up and said: 'Sergei, we are off to Cherliany, where the 127th Regiment of our division is based.' While I was refuelling my machine the regiment flew away. I took off – the German tanks were already approaching the aerodrome. I flew over the new aerodrome – there was a cross on the ground and bomb craters, still smoking: it was impossible to land. I flew over the CP – I used to land down there and knew where the CP was at this aerodrome. I landed and taxied over. I saw three planes from our regiment. Those were the guys who had returned from sorties before me.

After some time nine others landed. Work on aerodrome reconstruction began. And then eight Me-110s came over – no chance to take off under them! The Germans were attacking but what struck me most was that Petr Ganichev and his deputy, Colonel Matvei Zakharov, stood on the aerodrome field supervising the levelling work like idiots. Matvei Zakharov was hit in the forehead. Petr Ganichev was hit in the stomach and died two hours later. Now no commanders were left at the aerodrome . . .

The 127th Regiment was based at this aerodrome. It was equipped with I-153s armed with ShKAS machine-guns. Our I-16 had both 20mm ShVAK guns and 7,62mm ShKAS. But there were no shells for the cannons, so we fought with the ShKASes only. I shot down a Ju-88 [. . .] After all, I had been trained how to converge and I had approached him from below. Then I pulled up the machine and his engine caught fire. Apparently, I'd hit the pilot as well, because the plane fell straightaway. I reported my 'kill' but there was no HQ to confirm it, so it didn't count.

It was getting dusky, almost dark. And there's a command to 'relocate to Lida'. Our regiment was the first to take off. We flew over to Lida and landed. No fuel, no ammo. Actually, to be precise, everything was there, but the shells were covered in motor oil and the fuel tank was underground – but there were no pumps. Not even any buckets! We had some food and went to bed. We had just fallen asleep when the alarm sounded. They said that paratroopers had landed on the eastern side of the aerodrome. We ran to the aerodrome – the planes standing with empty tanks. What to do? No one knew anything. What to refuel the machines with? With nothing! And at that moment groups of six or eight Me-110s came over one after another – and both regiments were no more. And we could do nothing! There were airworthy planes down there but they were not fuelled or armed [. . .] An order came to quit. We went to the hotel, took our suitcases, and were taken to Moscow.[13]

Ganichev's decision to relocate the 122nd Regiment to Lida, in order to join divisional HQ and the 127th FAR, was valid – they had to leave an aerodrome that had been under attack. But the Lida airfield was a Luftwaffe target too, and, as Sergei Dolgoushin recounts above, Ganichev was mortally wounded by a bomb splinter. Nevertheless, pilots of the 122nd and the 127th FARs claimed the destruction of 17 Bf-109s, 11 Bf-110s and 7 Ju-88s during this intense period of air fighting. By the end of 22 June, the 122nd FAR had lost 69 I-16s (about half were destroyed on the Lida airfield). The 16th Bomber Aviation Regiment of the same 11th Aviation Division, which had lost 23 SBs and 37 Pe-2s on that day, was also ruthlessly routed.

During the first days of the war, a major problem for Soviet aviation units was the difficulty posed by manoeuvring between aerodromes. The origin of this problem has been highlighted above, with reference to the incomplete state of the Baltic Military District's rear-line aerodromes, which should have been ready to accept aviation units under threat at the border. It was the same situation in the Western Military District.

A retributive strike on enemy aerodromes was a key point in Nikolai Shpanov's influential pre-war novel, *The First Blow: A Novel of Future War* – a fictional scenario in which the USSR repels a German invasion with a single, powerful blow. Shpanov's colourful prose anticipated the destruction of the Luftwaffe within hours:

Enemy hangars were showered with incendiary bombs. The hit-rate was satisfactory despite good work by the enemy air defence. More than 50 per cent of his brand-new twin-cannon fighter planes had been destroyed on the ground before they had a chance to take off.[14]

One of Shpanov's biggest mistakes was his assessment of enemy ground services. In his novel, he predicted:

> despite the endurance of enemy airmen [. . .] their ground crews seemed incapable of getting them into the air [. . .] The first hours of hostilities revealed the social deficiencies of the enemy force, hidden by harsh discipline in peacetime. One should not forget that the auxiliary personnel – mechanics, electricians, and the dozens of other specialists required to service a combat plane – were just ordinary soldiers raised from industrial labourers. While German officers were eager to fly against the Soviet planes, the ground crews had their own opinion and showed less zeal. While Soviet bombers blasted [enemy] aerodromes, the ground services preferred to hide in shelters. [Repair] work at the aerodromes was performed more sluggishly than required by the situation. The impact of the very first Soviet bomb plainly confirmed the biggest problem for the German Command: the shortage of technical personnel. Too much depended on men with skilled and rough hands. There was simply too much that *Herr Offizier* could not do himself.[15]

Such emphasis on class division was typical for the pre-war Soviet propaganda machine. Essentially it was an attempt to locate an Achilles heel in an economically advanced foe. Needless to say, Nikolai Shpanov's expectations were never realised. While *Herr Offizier* might have been technically incapable of servicing his plane, he didn't have to, as every German plane was allocated a dozen technicians. And on 22 June these technicians were in no hurry to display proletarian class solidarity: rather, they tirelessly prepared aircraft for new sorties. And the technical perfection of German aviation facilitated a very high rate of operational sorties. Consequently, the total loss of the Western Front aviation was 738 planes on the first day of *Barbarossa* and of this number, 528 had been destroyed on the ground. The losses were mostly incurred by the 9th IAD (352 planes). Accordingly, the 10th IAD lost 180 planes, the 11th IAD 127 planes. Essentially, the Air Force of the Front had been destroyed. A harsh phrase concludes the destruction of the Air Force, depicted hot on the heels of the events, in the operations logbook of the Western Front:

> The Western Front Air Force Commander, General–Major Ivan Kopets – the main culprit of the destruction of the aircraft – apparently wishing to escape punishment, shot himself on the same evening of 22 June. Other offenders were to get their just rewards later.[16]

The 'other offenders' referred to above were most likely the 9th Aviation Division Commander, General Chernykh, and the Western Front Commander. They were quickly arrested and executed.

While the Western Special Military District bore the brunt of *Barbarossa*'s opening hours, the much stronger Kiev Special Military District was left virtually untouched. By the beginning of the war, this District fielded 2,003 combat aircraft, 1,759 of which were counted as airworthy. The District's Fighter Command consisted of seventeen aviation regiments, totalling 1,166 planes. The mainstay of the Bomber Command consisted of eleven short-range bomber regiments, numbering 468 planes. The District also had a long-range bomber aviation division, plus two ground–attack aviation regiments (mostly equipped with I-153s and I-15s), and two reconnaissance aviation regiments the (315th and the 316th). A further twelve aviation regiments – still being formed – were also stationed in the Kiev Special Military District. Organization and distribution of aviation regiments complied with the dominating concept regarding their operational role: thus, two–thirds of the District's aviation was placed at the disposal of Army commanders, leaving only one–third for the Front Command. Accordingly, if one of the armies was attacked, only the planes attached to that army, plus the Front Air Force, would be scrambled. Pulling air units from neighbouring armies was deemed 'problematical'.

The Luftwaffe's Air Fleet 4, assigned to support Army Group South, numbered more than 700 planes, making up 12 groups of bombers, 7 groups of fighters, 3 long-range reconnaissance squadrons, 2 groups of transport aviation and 3 signal squadrons. Commanded by General A. Löhr, Air Fleet 4 consisted of two Air Corps, the IV and V – the former was assigned to support the Eleventh German Army plus two Romanian armies; the latter to support the Sixth and Seventeenth Armies and 1st Panzer Group. In addition to these duties, Air Fleet 4 was also tasked with raiding the aerodromes of the Kiev and Odessa Military Districts.

In comparison to the other near-border districts, the aviation divisions stationed in the Ukraine put up the strongest resistance to the Luftwaffe. Why? First, the balance of power favoured the Kiev District. Second, the local Air Force Command, in the person of Evgeni Ptoukhin, had been paying attention to camouflaging the aerodromes. Shortly before the invasion, Evgeni Ptoukhin personally flew around the aerodromes, in order to check the implementation of the Narkom of Defence's order regarding camouflaging. Third, aerodromes in the Kiev District were well dispersed, so not all were hit on the first day of *Barbarossa*.

From 4 to 5 a.m. on 22 June, about 400 planes from the German V Air Corps struck 24 aerodromes of the Kiev Special Military District. It was mainly the near-border aviation divisions that found themselves under attack. Of six aerodromes belonging to the 14th Aviation Division (5th Army), five were bombed: Velitsk, Kolky, Kivertsy, Mlinov and Dubno. Attacks on aerodromes were even more intense in the Lwów Salient. A pilot of the 165th FAR, Sergei Gorelov, remembers:

> Three regiments concentrated at the Lwów aerodrome – about 200 planes. And just on my birthday, at 3 a.m., they began to bomb us. We all jumped up, ran to the aerodrome, but [. . .] Almost all the planes had been destroyed or damaged. My I-16 was not an exception. When I came up to her, it seemed to me as if she – lopsided, with torn the off left wing – was looking at me and asking: 'Where have you been? Why the hell were you sleeping?' [. . .] On the same day we were given vehicles and driven towards Kiev. While we drove through the Lwów Oblast, seven men were killed in our vehicle. The locals shot at us from bell towers, from garrets.

That was how much they hated us, the Soviets [. . .] And once the war started, they were not afraid of us any more.[17]

On the first day of the war, all aerodromes of the 15th and 63rd IAD, plus three out of four aerodromes of the 16th Aviation Division, were attacked from the air. Of course, the first strike was a surprise, even in a situation of heightened readiness for action. The commander of the 87th FAR, Major Ivan Souldin, remembers:

> On 22 June, about 4.30 a.m., our regiment received a cable from Divisional HQ: 'According to available information, German aviation is bombing the near-border cities of Przemysl, Rava–Russkaya and others. The regiment is to be made ready for action.' The acting regimental commander, Senior Lieutenant Mikhailyuk, roused the personnel by alarm. Airmen, engineers, technicians, junior aviation specialists, took their posts by the fighter planes according to the battle order; pilots from the 36th Aviation Division stood by the ten planes allotted to them and started engines. Seemingly, there was full combat readiness.
>
> But a serious blunder was made, for which many were to pay a heavy price. At about 4.50 a.m., a twin-engine bomber, poorly visible in the beams of the rising sun, came in sight from the east. Everyone thought that the Aviation Division Commander had flown over in an SB [bomber] to check the readiness of the regiment for action. But it was a German Ju-88 bomber. It attacked the planes parked in lanes. Having noticed the ominous black crosses on the bomber, commanders and soldiers opened rifle fire on it. But it was too late. The German plane precisely dropped small splinter bombs and strafed the personnel from machine-guns: out of ten lined-up planes, seven burned out; two pilots (who were in the cockpits) were killed, and two junior aviation specialists were wounded . . .[18]

Having come to its senses after the first strike, this regiment organized a permanent watch in the air above 87th FAR. The patrolling flight of Senior Lieutenant Dmitriev, based at Buchach, 60km south-east of Tarnopol, intercepted three Ju-88 bombers on the approach to the aerodrome at 5.30 a.m.

The Germans had even more success in their strikes on 'sleeping' aerodromes. Pilots of the 66th Ground Attack Aviation Regiment of the 15th Aviation Division (6th Army) considered the Sunday battle alarm as a drill and were late arriving at the aerodrome: this resulted in the loss of thirty-four machines – more than half of the regiment's aircraft. On weekends, pilots of the 17th FAR of the 14th Aviation Division (5th Army) would leave to see their families in Kovel. The Saturday of 21 June was no exception. Consequently, the regiment's aerodrome was pounded by German bombers with impunity the following day. Meanwhile, at Czernowitz (Czernowce) aerodrome, a hangar and twenty-one planes were destroyed.

In the first hours of *Barbarossa* German aviation was mainly opposed by fighter flights 'on watch', which took to the skies on a signal from a ground-based observation post. One such flight was led by a senior lieutenant with the pure Russian name of Ivan Ivanov. Having expended his ammunition while attacking a group of He-111s belonging to 3./KG 55, Ivanov rammed a bomber piloted by Werner Bahringer. Both planes fell to the ground in flames. This was the first of some 580 rammings performed by Soviet airmen during the war. Ivanov was awarded a posthumous Hero of the Soviet Union.

Meanwhile, Viktor Sinaisky, a motorist of the 131st FAR based near Krivoy Rog, remembered:

Moses Tokarev and Garmash lived separately, in the village, and all of us lived in tents near the aerodrome. On 22 June it was drizzling. The night was quiet. We slept in the tents to the accompaniment of the rain. Soon after sunrise, a howling siren resounded. We all began to grumble: 'Batya [i.e. 'Daddy' – obviously a nickname for the commander – trans.] doesn't want to let us relax, does he?! Only three days ago we were beating off a Romanian landing force [apparently a comment regarding drilling – trans.] and now there's another alarm!' I ran to the plane, removed the soft cover, started the engine, and began testing it. Other planes got their engines started too. The squadrons were parked on all sides of the rectangular airfield. Our squadron was closer to the village than the rest, and for that reason we were the first to get the engines going.

Soon, the other squadrons started their engines [. . .] When the fourth squadron got going, I was finishing off the engine test and had warmed it up. Suddenly, I felt as the control column was hitting me on the legs. I saw as the weapons engineer was jerking an aileron, showing me that I had to reduce throttle: so I did. He came up and said that the machine-guns needed a test. I was outraged – to conduct shooting [tests] from four machine-guns, then remove them and clean them up, would have taken half a day – the whole Sunday would have been stuffed. He said something else but I understood nothing. Then, he jabbed his hand at my shoulder, leaned to my ear and shouted: 'It's war, Sinaisky, war, what a Sunday!' And off he went. Of course, I revved up, for it was only possible to shoot at high speed, otherwise I might have shot through the prop blades from the synchronized machine-guns. I made shots from all four machine-guns, turned the engine off, got out, and awaited orders. At that moment, Garmash ran about. I have to say that, in the time of peace, we were interested in the combat experience obtained by these squadrons in Mongolia. Then, Garmash used to say that the first thing was to dig slit trenches without awaiting orders. You've got a free minute? Dig a trench – it'll save your life. Nothing's gonna protect you when bombers come over. It's gonna be even worse if there's a ground attack – only a slit trench will save you! So, without waiting for any instructions, we began to dig slit trenches. Then Moses Tokarev ran about – we stopped digging trenches for some time and dragged the planes to the belt of wood girding the aerodrome, and camouflaged them. Then we set on the trenches again. And by the time a German scout plane came over, as if the schedule, there were no signs of our presence at the aerodrome. Apparently, due to this, the Germans didn't touch our aerodrome on the first day of the war – all measures had been undertaken on time.[19]

But it would be wrong to assume the Germans' success was merely secured by the element of surprise. Many Soviet regiments were alert and managed to repulse the Luftwaffe's first strike in a fitting manner. For example, all airworthy fighter planes of the 164th FAR (15th Aviation Division) took off from the Kurovitze aerodrome to engage the enemy in the air. On the first day of *Barbarossa* pilots of the 164th Regiment shot down four German bombers and one fighter – despite being equipped with outdated aircraft like the I-16 ('Ishak') and I-153 ('Chaika'). Nevertheless, German consistency, perseverance and method paid off: if success was not achieved on the first raid, consecutive sorties were sure to bring the German airmen victory.

Meanwhile, in the Kiev Special Military District – where the balance of aviation numbers was in the defenders' favour – some aerodromes suffered no aerial attacks on the first days of the war. A technician from the 62nd Aviation Division, Alexander Boudouchev, recalled:

> The war began from the battle alarm at 3.30 a.m. The planes were quickly prepared for an operational sortie. Time went by but our planes flew nowhere and there were no flying personnel. Everyone thought it was just a regular drill. But when we saw large groups of unfamiliar aircraft flying eastwards, we became anxious – is it war? At 10 a.m. the order was announced that Fascist Germany had attacked us, and what our army had to do – in particular the aviation.[20]

A gunner from the 52nd Aviation Regiment of the same Aviation Division, Alexei Klochkov, tells:

> On 22 June 1941 we were raised by alarm at 4 a.m. We quickly got dressed, climbed into cockpits, warmed the engines up, and awaited the order to take off (thinking it was an ordinary drilling alarm). We waited for an hour, then two . . . We got out of the planes, made ourselves comfortable under a wing. At that time an armada of planes flew over the aerodrome at high altitude. Their silhouettes and formation were unfamiliar to us. We began to guess what kind of planes they were. Someone suggested they were new long-range bombers on manoeuvres. Only Captain Larionov, who had fought in Spain in his time [. . .], expressed doubts: 'For some reason I dislike these planes and their formation!'[21]

It was believed that the Kiev Military District lost 301 planes on the first day of *Barbarossa*, 174 of which were destroyed or damaged on the ground. However, new research reveals that some 277 Soviet aircraft were destroyed on the ground. This is a substantial figure, but the Western Special Military District lost many more aircraft on 22 June – a total of 738. Indeed, the Western Military District lost 41 per cent of its planes on that single day, while the Kiev Military District lost only 15.5 per cent.

The damage inflicted on the invader is the subject of lively discussion, even nowadays. According to an estimate by Russian historian Dmitri Khazanov, the German V Air Corps found thirty-five aircraft and twenty-seven crews missing on the first day of *Barbarossa*. A total of thirteen aircraft were mentioned as lost in the official history of the 55th Battle Wing, with seven crews killed or missing in action. Most of its Heinkel bombers were lost during an attack on the Mlynuv aerodrome, where they became victims of the I-16s and I-153s of the 14th Aviation Division (5th Army). The 51st Battle Wing incurred even higher losses: its logbook paints a sombre picture for 22 June 1941:

> After the last plane landed at 20.30 by the Polyanka Palace near Krosno, Kommodore Oberstleutnant Schulzhein summarized the results of that day: sixty men of the flying personnel [i.e. fifteen crews – ed.] have been killed or [are] missing in action, more than 50 per cent of all machines of the 3rd Group have been shot down or damaged.[22]

One shouldn't think that the air operations of the Southwestern Front were exclusively passive or defensive. The 62nd Aviation Division of the 5th Army bombed German battle formations near Ustilug. A navigator of the 94th Aviation Regiment, Alexander Kachanov, recalled:

> We took off about 4 p.m. from the Fosnya aerodrome (10km south of the City of Ovruch). The task for this sortie was to bomb a concentration of tanks, armoured vehicles and men on Polish territory, west of Vladimir-Volynsky. We approached the target at a height of 5,500m. We encountered strong flak before the target, which could be seen in flashes (I saw these

for the first time). There was a dogfight too. I saw with my own eyes as our I-16 attacked a Messerschmitt-109, which went down in smoke [. . .] I was on the right, in the first flight [of the regiment's formation]. The bomb bay opens, the bombs fly. At that moment, something came off the Regimental Commander's plane and flew down, glittering. After this, the Regimental Commander sharply turned right and descended below the formation – the prop of his right engine had been knocked off by a direct flak hit. Despite this, he made it to the aerodrome with one engine and landed, having flown about 350km.[23]

But the aerial battle over the Ukraine was only just beginning. Despite being badly beaten in the air and on the ground, the aviation divisions of the near-border armies had not lost their fighting spirit. And deep behind the lines of the Southwestern Front stood the fully intact 17th, 19th and 44th Aviation Divisions – their aerodromes suffered no air raids at all on 22 June. Consequently, German airmen were to encounter hundreds of planes from these 'deep-deployed' aviation units, so Luftwaffe air supremacy was out of the question on the first day of *Barbarossa*. True, German aviation held the initiative, but couldn't prevent Soviet strikes on troops at the front, or the significant role played by air units of the Southwestern Front in the tank battle in the Brody–Dubno area.

In the Odessa Military District, air activity on the first day of Operation *Barbarossa* was less intense than in the north, as the southern flank was a secondary consideration for both sides. The main strike force of Air Fleet 4 consisted of the 27th Battle Wing (KG 27) and the 77th Fighter Wing (JG 77). German aircraft numbers were augmented by Romanian assets, but opposing forces in this sector were fairly balanced.

The Germans struck at six aerodromes in the Odessa Military District, and the course of events was typical: a warning from Soviet observation posts launched a flight or squadron on watch. But Air Fleet 4 was much weaker than those operating at other sectors of the front, so strikes were less powerful, and Soviet patrols were capable of repulsing them.

An example is the action of the 55th FAR (20th Aviation Division) during an air raid on the Beltsy aerodrome between 5 and 6 a.m. on 22 June. Due to the timely warning from the observation posts, the squadron on watch (consisting of eight MiG-3s) took off immediately and engaged twenty He-111s and eighteen Bf-109s – the Germans only managed to damage three planes and set alight a small fuel depot. Meanwhile, the 4th FAR of the same division lost not a single plane on the ground over the course of ten air raids. But one shouldn't think that the 'Aerial Pearl Harbor' of *Barbarossa*'s first days had no effect on the Odessa Military District. The Commander of the 20th Aviation Division, Alexander Osipenko, highlighted a series of shortcomings in the action of his subordinates:

> 1. Despite possession of a sufficient amount of time between the alarm and the enemy air raid, the units failed to repulse the strike with minimum losses [. . .] and inflict damage on the enemy. The enemy retired unpunished and we suffered heavy losses on the ground due to criminal negligence and disorganization.
>
> 2. Dispersion of the materiel was unsatisfactory in all regiments. The planes are crammed; airworthy and inoperative planes stand on the same field.
>
> 3. It cannot be disguised – the situation in the 55th FAR is especially bad.[24]

However, unlike in Belorussia, there was no relentless air campaign against the aerodromes of the southern sector. The most modern Su-2 bombers, with which 210th and 211th Aviation Regiments of the Odessa Military District were armed, incurred no losses – on the ground or in the air. A Flight Commander of the 210th Short-Range Bomber Regiment, Alexander Pavlichenko, remembers:

> Sunday, 22 June [. . .] We were based at an aerodrome near Pervomaisk, the Pandurka Station – a field aerodrome. Then they woke us up and [. . .] at twelve o'clock they switched to Viacheslav Molotov's speech on the radio, announcing that the Germans had suddenly attacked us with no declaration of war.

We watched some planes flying at high altitude, but we didn't know who it was. The battle alarm was sounded. The planes were taxied to different spots, but the regiment was not ready for a sortie: there were no bomb-holders, no bombs; the planes were not refuelled; the weapons had not been charged with ammo. The commanders drove somewhere, and on their return the planes were immediately refuelled. And the first niner [i.e. formation of nine planes – ed.] was sent towards the border: I led the second flight in this niner; the Squadron Commander, the first; Lieutenant Gerashenko, the third. We arrived at the field aerodrome of Sofievka, which was about 70km from the border. But the bomb-holders and bombs were despatched to the spot only by evening, and at 18.46 we struck a railroad junction in Romania, Iasi – enemy territory. They were unloading freight cars, more than sixty trains. They were not expecting us, for they thought they'd just neutralized our aviation. [There were] lots of people around the trains. We converged at a low altitude – about 900m – a flak gun opened fire, flashing. For the first time in our lives we saw flak shells bursting. We set on a strike course and opened bomb bays [. . .] No fighter planes attacked us over the target, only a flak gun fired. Then we turned around and headed towards our aerodrome. We arrived there but there was none of our fighter-planes anymore. We were ordered to leave the aerodrome straightaway. The night was coming. We filled the tanks with as much fuel as possible and relocated to another aerodrome near Voznesensk. Such was my first combat sortie. In the evening the Regimental Commander, Alexander Kozhemyakin, summoned us and said: 'You were lucky, you made it back with no losses.' Twenty-seven planes from the 45th IAD hadn't made it home. Mostly they were SBs. They'd flown to bomb different targets. And they'd flown to Iasi before us. There had been dogfights – the fighter-planes made it home. Not all of these twenty-seven were shot down: some had been shot up and landed on our own territory. Then it turned out that some had returned, but the division had lost twelve crews. Such was the beginning of the war for the 210th Regiment.[25]

It was a similar situation for the 211th Bomber Aviation Regiment in Kotlovsk. On the evening of 22 June, eight Su-2s made a sortie to bomb a crossing over the Prut, in the Lipkani–Dumeni area. The bombers incurred no losses (the first Su-2 was lost only on the 24 June). The crossings over the Prut were a popular target with the aircraft of the Odessa Military District: on the first day of *Barbarossa* seventeen Pe-2s destroyed the Galati Bridge across the Prut with bombs.

The Odessa District's aircraft losses for the first days of the war – while not as high as other sectors of the front – still look serious enough. According to German data, Luftwaffe crews shot down sixteen Soviet planes and destroyed 142 more on the ground. For their part, the Soviet Command only admitted a loss of twenty-three planes. The truth is probably somewhere in the middle – perhaps the Odessa Military District lost no less than forty or fifty planes.

The Soviet Long-Range Bomber Aviation (LRBA) suffered least of all from the aerodrome raids on 22 June. Its bases were far from the border and were not attacked on the first day of the war (the first raids occurred on 23 June). For this reason, *Barbarossa*'s overture was quiet for the units of the LRBA. The 3rd Heavy Bomber Regiment, located closer to the border than any other LRBA unit, provides a characteristic example. The concrete airstrip of its main base at Borovichy was under reconstruction and, since it was the time of summer camp, the regiment relocated to a reserve 'field' airfield nearby. Early on 22 June, the camp was roused by alarm. The squadron commanders were ordered to HQ for an urgent dispatch. However, having arrived, the commanders found no one there – the building was empty. They stood, perplexed, for some time, then returned to their tents to resume their interrupted dreams. But they understood that war had begun even before Viacheslav Molotov's speech: a dense pillar of smoke was seen rising over the horizon in the direction of Minsk. Nikolai Bogdanov, a pilot of 212th LRBA Regiment, recalled:

At the time when near-border units of the Red Army repulsed the first Fascist attacks, our regiment (based at the Smolensk aerodrome) was preparing for a sortie in the morning haze. When the planes with tested engines, fixed up bombs, charged machine-guns were ready to take off, all crews were lined up at the aerodrome [. . .] Time and again during that stressful day we received operational tasks that were later cancelled [or] objectives and bomb-loads were changed. But we [made no] sortie on the first day of the war.[26]

Soviet strategic bombers received their orders in the second half of the day (targets in Poland, Germany and Romania had been contemplated before the war), and some aviation regiments took off westwards. The 1st LRBA Corps bombed Königsberg and Tilsit. Sorties against the invading land forces on Soviet territory were set up too. The clumsy DB–3F carried out these tasks without fighter escort. The Commander of the 3rd LRBA Corps, Nikolai Skripko, remembered his first sortie of the war like this:

At 13.40 on 22 June the Commander of the 207th Regiment, Lieutenant-Colonel Titov, and his wingmen, were the first to take off [. . .] The Commander was followed by Captain Kozlov with his subordinates, Senior Lieutenants Koshel'kov, Moul'tanovsky, Chistyakov and other flight commanders. Lieutenant-Colonel Titov quickly gathered his units and headed westwards. Cumulus clouds began to form. The flights dipped under the clouds according to the estimated time schedule. In the Merkani area they discovered a large motorized enemy column, stretched over many kilometres, and at 15.40 hours the leading flight struck the enemy, bombing from a height of 1,000m (well aimed and precise). Direct hits on enemy armoured vehicles and motorcars were observed. Others followed the Commander's example. Then the aviation regiment bombed another German column, which was approaching the settlement of Leptuni. The bombs struck the centre of the column. During the second approach, from a height of 600m and lower, our crews strafed the [enemy] with machine-gun fire.[27]

The sortie made by the 96th LRBA Regiment occurred in more difficult conditions. As the unit Commander, Andrei Mel'nikov, had returned from vacation only on the second day of the war, the regiment's first operational sortie was headed by his deputy, Major Andrei Slepoukhov. He led twenty-nine crews and bombed motorized enemy columns from a height of 1,200–1,500m in the area of Seini–Suwałki–Augustów–Kvitemotis. At the approaches to small bridges there where significant concentrations of German tanks, motorized infantry and artillery. The Squadron Commander, Senior Lieutenant Bourykh, the Flight Commander, Lieutenant Ivan Kaplya, and their wingmen inflicted heavy losses on the enemy.

Our bombers were fired on from small-calibre flak guns and attacked by Me-109 fighters on many occasions. After the aerial gunner, Khabalov, had repulsed a 109's attack with a long burst from the upper-turret machine-gun, the enemy fighter tried to attack the Il-4 bomber from below, from the tail side. In the past, this semi-sphere had been poorly protected, so the enemy didn't realise that now there was an extra machine-gun in that place. Khabalov managed to man this gun and sent a burst. The Fascist fighter fell to the ground in flames. But we lost three planes on that day too, including the bomber commanded by Lieutenant Ivan Grigorievich Kaplya. During an unequal fight against the German fighters, his machine was badly damaged. Fuel began to leak from a shot-through tank and the plane caught fire. By the order of the Commander, all crew members abandoned the burning bomber. Lieutenant Kaplya was the last to bail out. Having swum across several rivers and overcome numerous obstacles and adversities, he made it back to our lines. And the Lieutenant's first request was to let him make a combat sortie!

On 22 June the 98th LRBA Regiment of the 52nd Aviation Division operated in a more southern direction. Thirty-one crews, led by the Regimental Commander, Lieutenant-Colonel Shelest, headed along the Osipovichy – Pruzany – Janów line, with the task of bombing concentrations of tanks and motorized infantry on the roads between Janów, Luków, Sedlec, Biela-Podlaska. The crews went into the air after a short meeting, during which the pilots, navigators, aerial gunners, swore to give all their strength – and if need be their lives as well – to defend the Soviet Motherland [. . .] Having discovered in the assigned area columns of Fascist tanks and motorized infantry moving east, the flights of Il-4 planes bombed the concentrations of Hitlerites. The crews were attacked by groups of enemy fighters over the target and on the way back.

In the evening [. . .] I arrived at the Borovskoye aerodrome. Many planes had come back damaged; crewmen had been killed and wounded. Since one medical vehicle was not enough, trucks had to be used to transport the wounded men. Some damaged bombers couldn't taxi, but there were not enough retrievers to tow them. Then they began to use tractors – the most powerful special machines. Twenty-two Il-4s out of seventy that made their first operational sortie did not make it home. Apart from that, one bomber of the 96th Regiment exploded with his own FAB-1000 bomb: the pilot had 'jerked-up' his plane too early at take-off.[28]

In the evening of 22 June, the first Soviet night air-raid took place: the 53rd LRBA Regiment attacked the East Prussian seaport of Königsberg. Having highlighted the target with illumination bombs, the flyers dropped their load and caused several fires.

When evaluating the results of the aerial battle of 22 June 1941 it is impossible not to recall the words of Pavel Rychagov at the meeting of December 1940 (referred to at the beginning of the chapter): 'Most of these raids will fail.' Indeed, German airmen frequently failed on the first or even second raid; moreover, some Soviet aerodromes of the near-border districts were destroyed only on the second or third day of the war. Nevertheless, German persistence – and Soviet unpreparedness – permitted the Luftwaffe to achieve tangible air dominance, if not complete mastery. The annihilation of many Soviet aircraft on the ground, on the very first day of *Barbarossa* nullified the Red Air Force's initial numerical superiority. And heavy losses among Soviet fighters left bomber squadrons without escorts – they would pay a bloody price for every strike against German armoured columns. However, due to the Luftwaffe's concentrated efforts in the skies of Belorussia, in support of *Barbarossa*'s main strike, the Red Air Force retained its fighting capacity in the Ukraine, further south. Indeed, the Kiev District's aviation was actively engaged in near-border battles, deterring German advances in the Ukrainian sector; and efficient aerial reconnaissance facilitated accurate responses from the Soviet Command, staving off the threat of collapse.

Photo Album:
Barbarossa Maintained

A KV-2 tank, presumably from the 16th Tank Regiment (8th Tank Division), at the southern outskirt of Nemiroff, 25–28 June 1941.

A 152mm ML-20 howitzer in the sector of advance of the 97th Light Infantry Division (Army Group South), June 1941.

A BT-7 tank burned out during the attack on Nemiroff (1st Platoon, 1st Company, 53rd Tank Regiment, 81st Motorized Division).

Abandoned during the retreat from Lwów—a T-28 tank (with hand-held antenna around the turret) from the 8th Tank Division (4th Motorized Corps), Lychakovskaya Street, Lwów, 24 June 1941.

A T-34 tank from the 15th Tank Regiment (8th Tank Division), abandoned by its crew after the attack on Nemiroff (Western Ukraine), 24 June 1941.

Two KV-2 tanks from the 8th Tank Division (4th Mechanized Corps), abandoned and blasted in the sector of advance of the 97th Light Infantry Division (Army Group South), June 1941, north-west of Lwów.

A KV-1 tank abandoned in a park, June 1941.

A KV-2 tank of the 15th Tank Regiment (8th Tank Division, 4th Motorized Corps) abandoned during the retreat from Lwów.

Red Army column destroyed by air raids on the Lwów–Zolochev road, near the village of Yasenovtsy. In the photos a 152mm M-10 howitzer, a KV-2 tank, tractors and a ZIS truck can be seen.

A T-34 tank from the 15th Tank Regiment (8th Tank Division, 4th Mechanized Corps) burned out as a result of action against the 97th Light Infantry Division near Magerov on 25 June 1941.

KV-1 tank with the L-11 gun from the 12th Tank Division, 8th Mechanized Corps of the Southwestern Front (presumably the 23rd Tank Regiment) after an action against the 100th Light Infantry Division in Nikolayev, Lvovskaya Oblast. This tank, together with a KV-2 tank, blocked the central square and delayed the enemy advance for 3 hours. The tank's turret is jammed and the gun barrel shot through. Its crew fought a close and fatal action outside the tank, dying on 1 July 1941.

A T-34 tank with F-34 gun from the 32nd Tank Division (4th Mechanized Corps), shot up near the village of Yazyv Stary (60km west of Lwów) on 25–26 June

T-34 and BT-5 tanks abandoned in a park, most likely due to their technical condition.

A ZK 76mm AA gun, 1931 model (location unknown).

A burned out T-40 tank (location unknown).

A destroyed T-28 tank (most likely from the 10th Tank Division) in Zolochev, 1–2 July 1941.

A shot-up, radio-equipped T-34 (location unknown).

AT-35 tank from the 67th Regiment (34th Tank Division) in Grodek Yagel'onsky, Western Ukraine, June 1941.

A burned-out BA-10 armoured car on the road before Holosko, 29–30 June 1941.

These three photographs show the trophy ground of the German troops in Yavorov, following an action against units of the 6th Rifle Division and the 4th Mechanized Corps, which took place on 24–26 June.

A BT-7 tank with P-40 AA fire system and combat spotlights (most likely from the 1st Tank Division) near Pskov.

Abandoned BT-2 and BT-5 tanks near Rovno (Western Ukraine). The tanks had been reconditioned, equipped with logs for self-pulling (BT-2) and additional fuel tanks (BT-5).

Abandoned T-26 tank (1939 series). The white crosses on the opened turret hatches are aerial identification markings used on the Northwestern Front.

Fallen soldiers. The half-empty cartridge belt in the Maxim machine-gun tells us that these soldiers fulfilled their duty to the last.

Fallen soldier. In the lower right corner of the photo is a stick of five RGD grenades for use against German armour.

Body-search of
a POW.

A POW
watching a
Stug III firing.

Women were
also among the
volunteers.

In a few days war changed the lives of all ordinary people. Young men stick a propaganda poster on the wall. The girl caries a poster 'Be a hero!'

'Our tobacco will help fighters beat the enemy!'

Chapter 7

. . . And at Sea

The summer of 1941 was not the best time for the German Kriegsmarine: the *Bismark* battleship had been sunk; her sister ship, *Tirpitz*, had not yet reached the open sea; the heavy cruiser *Prinz Eugen* was blockaded at Brest; the cruiser *Lützow* had been put out of action for months by a torpedo hit; the heavy cruisers *Admiral Hipper* and *Admiral Scheer* were undergoing repairs. Out of four light cruisers, only *Nürnberg* and *Köln* were fully seaworthy. As to the Black Sea, the Germans couldn't physically place large surface ships there, so it would have been imprudent to task the Kriegsmarine with destroying the Soviet Navy. Nevertheless, the Soviet Navy couldn't be ignored – Germany depended on shipping (primarily iron ore from Sweden), so to guarantee secure supplies, it was necessary to blockade enemy ships at their bases. The simplest way of doing this was laying minefields.

The German Command managed to make life easier by securing the support of Finland. Without the availability of Finnish bases, blockading the Gulf of Finland with mines would have entailed German ships crossing the whole Baltic from south to north, thus compromising secrecy. The German minelayers received orders to conduct the operation on 8 June 1941. The first group, code-named 'Kobra' (consisting of the vessels *Kobra*, *Königin Luize* and *Kaiser*), left Danzig on 12 June and – posing as merchantmen – anchored near Helsinki late on 14 June. Finnish pilots and liaison officers joined the German crewmen during the night. The second group, code-named 'Nord' (consisting of the vessels *Tannenberg*, *Brummer* and *Hanzestadt Danzig*), sailed from Pillau on 12 June – again, under the false colours of the German merchant marine.

On 14/15 June, the German ships, assisted by Finnish pilots, dropped anchor near Turku (Abo). The Germans also assigned torpedo boats to the mine-laying operation. These 'boats' were actually substantial vessels, and their use as minelayers should not come as a surprise. On 18 June, torpedo boats of the 1st Flotilla moored at a base near Helsinki. On the same day, boats from the 2nd Flotilla arrived at Turku. These two flotillas had previously been operating in the English Channel and had considerable combat experience. Another group of German vessels that sailed into Finnish waters consisted of twelve minesweepers with the tender ship *Elbe*. This flotilla left Hotenhaven (the naval base at Danzig) on 15 June and, having split into two groups, arrived at bases near Turku and Helsinki. Everything was ready for the implementation of a large-scale operation to block shipping routes out of the Gulf of Finland.

The German mine-laying operation began at 10.59 p.m. on 21 June – 4 hours prior to the commencement of hostilities on land. Hundreds of EMS mines and mine-sweeping obstacles were deployed in several 'screens'. By 4 a.m. the minelayers were heading back to their bases – but their activities had not escaped the attention of Soviet observers. A post on Naissar Island was the first to spot a group of ships heading south-west from Helsinki. However, due to the absence of naval patrols and aerial reconnaissance at the approaches to Tallinn, there was no opportunity for further scouting, and the situation remained unclear. And the report from Naissar was not the only one: at 1.50 a.m. on 22 June, the Tahkuna and Kypu posts on Dago Island spotted five ships sailing with no lights. Finally, at 3.30 a.m., the crew of a Soviet reconnaissance plane (Senior Lieutenant Troupov and Lieutenant Pouchkov from the 44th Special Reconnaissance Squadron) identified 'three destroyers and six launches' 20 miles north of the Tahkuna lighthouse. German destroyers had not been allocated for the operation – evidently the airmen had misidentified the minelayers. Nevertheless, the 'destroyers' opened fire at the plane: thus, the first shots of the Great Patriotic War were fired over the waves of the Baltic.

The Finns, meanwhile, not only provided bases and pilots to aid the German operation, they also laid mines (via submarines) in the immediate vicinity of the Estonian shoreline, as agreed at a conference with the German Command, held on 6 June 1941. The Finns would also prosecute their own naval campaign on 21/22 June, occupying the Åland Islands (declared a demilitarized zone following the Soviet–Finnish war of 1940) in Operation 'Regatta'. Taking full advantage of *Barbarossa*, the Finns landed 5,000 soldiers on the islands, supported by artillery and warships. The thirty-one members of the Soviet consulate were deported, arriving at Turku on 25 June.

Of course, the transformation of the Gulf of Finland and Baltic Sea into a terrible 'soup with dumplings' did not occur overnight. However, the pattern of naval warfare – in which mines were to play the major role – was already apparent on the first day of the war, and mines would take a heavy toll on all participants.

During Soviet times it was alleged that the report by the Naissar post (mentioned above) prompted the Navy to action stations. However, considering the time necessary to convey information from Naissar to N.G. Kouznetsov (Narkom of the Navy), the latter could only have got the news at 1 a.m. at best. Nevertheless, by 11.50 p.m. on 21 June, Kouznetsov had issued the directive: 'Switch to Operational Readiness No. 1 immediately' – i.e. before the discovery of enemy ships by the Naissar post. According to the operational dispatch of the Baltic Naval HQ, the following naval patrols were at sea at 8 p.m. on 21 June:

- In the Irben Straight: the *S-7* submarine, the *T-297* minesweeper (*Virsaitis*)
- In the mouth of the Gulf of Finland: the *M-99* submarine, the *T-216* minesweeper
- At the approaches to Tallinn: the guard-boat No. 141 and the *T-213* minesweeper
- At the approaches to Kronstadt: the guard-boats No. 223 and No. 224
- At the approaches to Liepaja: the guard-boats No. 214 and No. 212

During the last hours before *Barbarossa*, the ships of the Baltic Fleet executed the following movements: the battleship *Marat*, the guard-ships *Toucha*, *Sneg*, *Shtil*, and the minesweepers *T-203*, *T-205* and *T-201* arrived at Kronstadt. The minesweeper *T-204* was on its way from Tallinn to Liepaja. The battleship *Oktyabr'skaya Revolutsya*, the destroyers *Karl Marx* and *Volodarsky*, and the 2nd Division of minesweepers were busy drilling near Liepaja, off the Latvian coast. A detachment of light naval forces was at Ust-Dvinsk.

The Narkom of the Soviet Navy, N.G. Kouznetsov, was informed of the Kremlin's decision to rouse troops of the Special Military Districts by alarm:

> At about 11 p.m. the telephone rang. I heard the voice of Marshal S.K. Timoshenko: 'There is very important information. Come to see me.' Armed with the latest data on the situation in the fleets, I went [to Timoshenko] with Alafouzov. Vladimir Antonovich took the maps along with him. We planned to report the situation at the naval theatres. I saw Alafouzov examining his white tunic – he probably thought it inconvenient to visit the Narkom of Defence in such an outfit: 'Would be better to have something newer,' he joked. But there was no time to change.
>
> Our *Narkomat* (Narodnyi Commissariat – trans.) buildings stood nearby. We went outside. The rain had stopped and couples were strolling on the pavement again – people were dancing somewhere and the sound of a gramophone floated from an open window. Within minutes we were climbing the stairs of the small mansion where Timoshenko's office was located. The Marshal was striding across the office, dictating. It was still hot. General G.K. Zhukov sat at a desk, writing. Several sheets from a large notepad for radiograms lay in front of him. It was obvious that the Narkom of Defence and the Chief of staff had been working some time.
>
> Semen Konstantinovich noticed us and stopped. Without naming the source, he said a German attack on our country was imminent. Zhukov stood up and showed us a cable he had prepared for the near-border districts. I remember that it was verbose, taking up three sheets. It stated in detail what to do in case of attack. This cable didn't directly concern the fleets. Having quickly scanned the text of the cable, I asked: 'Is it permitted to use arms in case of attack?'

'It is.'

I turned to Rear-Admiral Alafouzov: 'Run to HQ and immediately send a directive on full practical readiness to the fleets – Operational Readiness No. 1. Run!' Back then, there was no time to reason if it was convenient for an admiral to run down a street.[1]

Meanwhile, in Tallinn, all was quiet. Yu. S. Roussin, who served in an 'M' type (nicknamed 'Malyutka' or 'Baby' – trans.) submarine, recalls the evening of Saturday, 21 June 1941:

> No one would have assumed this was the last day of peace, that the next would be a turning point in everyone's life, in the life of the country.
>
> At 23.37 hours, loud bells sounded in the ships. I have to note that we had heard such signals quite often and had got used to them. Back on 19 June, the Baltic Navy had been switched to Operational Readiness No. 2. In the past there'd been drilling alarms and the crew would do its duties in an established sequence. But this time the battle alarm put us on guard. It echoed in everyone's heart. And indeed, on that night, the Navy was switching to Operational Readiness No. 1.
>
> All night long, the crews of 'Malyutka' submarines stayed awake, awaiting the battle order. Many suspected that extraordinary events were to come . . . [2]

Kouznetsov, however, not content with ordering Operational Readiness No. 1, began telephoning each of the fleet commanders in turn – beginning with the Baltic Fleet and ending with the Black Sea Fleet at about 1 a.m. Kouznetsov also issued a more detailed directive:

> A sudden German attack on 22–23 June is possible. The German assault may start from provocative activities. Our duty is not to fall for any provocative actions that may cause major complications. At the same time the fleets and flotillas must be ready to repulse possible German strikes. My instructions are as follows: having switched to Operational Readiness No. 1, continue preparing for action in a covert manner. Reconnaissance in foreign territorial waters is strictly

forbidden. No other measures are to be undertaken without a special directive.[3]

Kouznetsov's previous order – simple and clear to all – was now replaced with the bewildering charge 'not to fall for any provocative actions' while 'preparing for action in a covert manner': a combination that, in the transition from peace to war, might have led to disastrous consequences. Luckily, the Soviet Navy was not a priority target for German aviation during *Barbarossa*'s first hours.

At 1.55 a.m. on 22 June, Vice-Admiral Ivan Eliseev, the Black Sea Fleet's Chief of Staff, decided to take the initiative and announced a 'grand gathering'. Now secrecy was out of the question: sirens began to howl and coastal batteries began to rumble. It had been quite an acceptable decision for a base situated deep in the rear. Eliseev also undertook to protect Sevastopol from aerial attack, ordering a general blackout. The pitch-darkness hid the bustling of hundreds of people, as ships took extra ammunition, torpedoes and other supplies onboard, and coastal batteries prepared their guns for live shells. At 3 a.m. on 22 June, the 61st Anti-aircraft Artillery Regiment, four battalions of coastal defence, and one squadron of the 32nd FAR reported full battle readiness.

Although more than an hour had elapsed since Eliseev's announcement of the 'grand gathering', making the ships ready for combat was lagging behind. But there was no time left for meditation. He-111s from the II Group, 4th Battle Wing, were approaching Sevastopol – from five to nine of them, according to various sources. These bombers were tasked with dropping mines in the outlet of Sevastopol's Northern Bay and, for increased psychological effect, they were supposed to do this in full view. But Eliseev's blackout significantly disorientated the German airmen and two mines were dropped on land, detonating at 3.48 a.m. and 3.52 a.m. respectively.

At 4.35 a.m., the Fleet Commander, F.S. Oktyabr'sky, ordered minesweeping operations, but the result was disappointing and alarming: no mines were found. Soviet vessels were only equipped to detect common contact mines but the Germans had dropped the latest non-contact magnetic mines: the first victim would be the Soviet towboat, *SP-12*, which, searching for a plane apparently downed by flak, exploded and sank in Karantinnaya Bay at 8.20 p.m.

on 22 June. Twenty-six crewmen perished and five were rescued. It would not be till 24 June – following the discovery of an unexploded German mine dropped on land – that the true nature of the minefield menace was revealed.

At 6 a.m. on 22 June, N.G. Kouznetsov ordered the Baltic and Black Sea Fleets to carry out defensive mine-laying operations. Despite the alacrity of this initiative, Kouznetsov's orders were not actioned until 23 June (in the Gulf of Finland) and 24 June (in Irben Bay). The laying of a defensive mine screen near Sevastopol commenced on 23 June and was completed on the 25th.

At 9.29 a.m. on 22 June, N.G. Kouznetsov sent the Black Sea Fleet a directive on the deployment of submarines:

Dispatch submarines to:

1) The area between Constanta and Sulina.

2) The area between Constanta and Burgas inclusive without penetration into the territorial waters of Bulgaria and Turkey.

The task: to cut communications, to target exclusively cargo ships and Romanian and German naval ships. Submarines must not be placed at the close approaches to Constanta and Sulina in the light of oncoming operations by surface ships.

Of course, the Black Sea Fleet was unable to send huge packs of submarines to the allocated positions. A significant number of Soviet submarines based on the Black Sea were not ready for immediate action on 22 June. Some were still being constructed, others were under repair in Sevastopol and Nikolayev. In fact, eighteen out of forty-seven submarines of the Black Sea Fleet were under repair; two were at the stage of organization with crews yet unprepared for action; two were in the training submarine division in Novorossisk. Consequently, only five submarines were operational on the first day of the war.

Patrol areas had been allocated before the war and, on the outbreak of hostilities, Soviet submarines deployed, ready to strike enemy vessels from under the water. The 'Malyutka' class submarines were placed at the western and south-western approaches to Sevastopol. At 7.35 p.m. on 22 June the submarine *M-33* went on patrol south-west of the Tarkhankout Cape (position

No. 1). At 8.28 p.m. an identical 'Malyutka' submarine, *M-34*, went on patrol south-west of the Sarych Cape (position No. 2). The other three positions to which Black Sea Fleet submarines were to be sent were near the Romanian coast. At 6.09 p.m. the submarine *Sh-205* took up position near Olin'ka Cape (position No. 3). At 6.24 p.m. the submarine *Sh-206* went on patrol towards the Shabler Cape (position No. 4). At 7.08 p.m. the submarine *Sh-209* went on patrol near the Emine Cape (position No. 5). Submarine *Sh-206* was the unluckiest one: she never made it home from the patrol and forty-five crew members were lost. Yet there is no evidence the submarine perished on the first day of the war: rather, it is believed that *Sh-206* was sunk on 9 July 1941 by Romanian surface vessels near the Tuzla lighthouse. That said, it might have struck a mine or suffered a technical failure or crew error. The other submarines did not encounter the enemy during their first wartime patrol.

Among the Baltic Soviet naval bases there was one located in the immediate vicinity of the border at the Latvian port of Liepaja. Consequently, the Germans didn't need Panzers to break through to it. On the morning of 22 June, units of the Wehrmacht's 291st Infantry Division, led by General Kurt Herzog, crossed the State Border. By 9 a.m. they had dislodged the local Soviet border guards from Palanga and threatened the approaches to Liepaja.

As of 22 June 1941, elements of the 1st, 3rd and 4th Submarine Divisions, the 1st Division of Minesweepers, five torpedo boats and thirteen patrol ships were based at Liepaja. But most of the submarines were outdated 'Malyutka' class vessels or old tubs belonging to the ex-Baltic states. Although it has been said that Liepaja was crammed with the Soviet submarines like a 'barrel of herrings', it was, at best, a 'barrel of sprats'. Apart from the submarines, an old destroyer, *Lenin*, was undergoing maintenance at Liepaja's 'Tosmar' shipyard. On the night of 21 June – several hours before the first German bombardment – the base minesweeper, *T-204*, called in at Liepaja for maintenance. Apart from naval ships there were also nineteen transports in port.

General-Major N.A. Dedaev's 67th Rifle Division protected Liepaja on land, but a huge stretch of coastline – from the State Border to Ventspils – was in its zone of responsibility: only some 7,000 men from Dedaev's command were stationed in the Liepaja area. Dedaev's force was augmented by other units: the 32nd Sentry Battalion of Naval Air Defence School cadets; the 23rd and 27th Batteries of Baltic Fleet Coastal Defence (four 130mm guns apiece); the 18th Railway Battery (four 180mm guns) of the Baltic Navy; the 148th FAR of the 6th IAD (sixty-three planes); the 43rd Naval Reconnaissance Squadron (consisting of thirteen MBR-2 flying boats, based at Lake Durbe, 15–20km from the city); and some other small units. The naval base personnel numbered about 4,000. The relatively small garrison at Liepaja's defence perimeter could repel the first enemy assault but as the prospects for prolonged resistance were vague. The only option for seaworthy ships was to sail to the Gulf of Riga.

The switch to Operational Readiness No. 1 was quickly implemented in Liepaja. At 4 a.m. N.I. Egipko – Commander of the 1st Submarine Brigade – received an order from Baltic Fleet HQ to take aboard all kinds of provisions and scatter his submarines along the river. Egipko was also instructed to relocate submarines of the 4th Division to Ust-Dvinsk, and those of the 3rd Division to Vindava. Petr Grishenko, commander of the *L-3* mine-laying submarine, recalls:

> The German attack on the Soviet came so suddenly that, when at 4 a.m. on 22 June, we saw aircraft above us marked with Swastikas, we assumed it was an exercise. The evening before, everyone heard the loudspeakers from the naval base repeating: 'Citizens! Local anti-aircraft drilling is in progress. Observe blackout procedures.' But at 11.37 p.m. [21 June] Operational Readiness No. 1 was announced for the Baltic Fleet. At 2 a.m. [22 June] naval personnel left the coastal barracks for the submarines. For the first hour onboard, me and the *zampolit* [i.e. political officer – trans.] stood on the bridge, smoked, and made guesses at what would happen. It was the same in the other submarines: everyone was waiting for 'lights-out', but it was not coming . . .
>
> Having descended to the central station, I decided not to waste time and to run survival and floodability drills. At 3.30 a.m., in the middle of this drilling, having received a radiogram

[from Fleet Commander Tributz] addressed to the whole Fleet, I quickly read aloud: 'Recently, commanding officers have been speculating on the possibility of war with Germany, and even guessing on the date of its onset [. . .] I order such gossiping to cease and [to] use every day, every hour, to intensify combat and political drilling.' Everyone sighed with relief. But two minutes later, Petrov, the navigator, reported from the bridge: 'Three bomber aircraft with black crosses and Swastika markings flew over the harbour at a height of 500–600m.'

I ordered the air-raid alarm and readied the AA gun for combat. But, bearing in mind the Fleet Commander's directive not to open fire, none of the submarine commanders had the courage to breach it. In the meantime, the aircraft flew over a third time. In the distance we heard explosions and gunfire . . .[4]

Preparations for the relocation took several hours, but, on 22 June, the Soviet seamen were not mainly concerned with the retreat from Liepaja. The *L-3*, *M-79*, *M-81* and *M-83* submarines were immediately sent to positions at the approaches to the base, which they were meant to take up according to the pre-war plans. *M-83* left Liepaja at 09.30 hours, *M-81* at 10.30 and *L-3* at 19.30. Despite engine problems, the *Fougas* minesweeper laid a screen consisting of 207 mines at the approaches to Liepaja. Although minesweepers of this design were primarily designed to eliminate enemy mines, they could also lay a small quantity of mines. The mine laying conducted by *Fougas* was to become quite effective: the German minesweepers *M3134*, *M1708* and *M1706*, the patrol vessel *V309* and the anti-submarine ship *UJ113* struck its mines before the end of 1941.

When the first artillery salvoes rumbled in the approaching darkness of the summer night, the order to evacuate was carried out. Thus, at 23.20 hours on 22 June, the *S-9*, *Kalev* and *Lembit* submarines left the base and sailed towards Vindava, followed by the *M-77* and *M-78* submarines after midnight. *M-78* was sunk by the German submarine *U-144* during the relocation. The *Fougas* minesweeper and several small 'hunters' left the base on 23 June. The tanker *Zheleznodorozhnik* and eight freight ships also quit port. The destroyer *Lenin* and submarines *Ronis*, *Spidola*, *M-71*, *M-80* and *S-1* would be scuttled to prevent their capture by the enemy.

The same fate befell the submarine *M-83*, which had returned to the base due to a damaged periscope. A train packed with the garrison's families left Liepaja on 23 June, along with the railway battery. The defence of Liepaja lasted till 27 June, although some dispersed detachments held out till 29 June.

As might be expected, the tally of Soviet civilian vessels sunk by the Germans was opened on 22 June, the steamship *Gaisma* (3007 GRT) being the first. It was en route from Riga to Lübeck with a cargo of timber. At 3.45 a.m. it was attacked by the German torpedo boats *S-59* and *S-60* near Gogland Island. The Germans shelled the vessel then sunk it with two torpedoes: six men were killed and two were taken prisoner. The remaining twenty-four crewmen reached the Latvian shore in a lifeboat, near the Uzhava lighthouse, where they buried Captain N.G. Duve, who had died of wounds. The freight ship *Liiza*, bound from Liepaja to Paldiski with a cargo of cement and barbed wire, was another victim. At 23.15 p.m. on 22 June it was detained by vessels of the German 2nd Flotilla near Dago Island. The Germans allowed the crew to leave the vessel, which was subsequently torpedoed by the *S-43* and *S-106* boats. The crew members (fourteen men and one woman) were taken into captivity aboard *S-106*.

Traditionally, the Soviet Navy has been favourably contrasted with the Army and Air Force with regard to battle-readiness. But in all fairness it must be noted that the Soviet Navy did not loom large in the Germans' *Barbarossa* plan. Nevertheless, 22 June might still have become a 'Day of Infamy' for the Red Navy, when German submariners discovered the battleship *Oktyabr'skaya Revolutsya* moored in the port of Tallinn. The German submarine commander, Captain Birnbacher, radioed for permission to attack. Approval came from the German base at Westende but Birnbacher's vessel was unable to pick up the message. Birnbacher called the base several times with the same result – and so a lucky set of circumstances saved the battleship. When one considers that Soviet ships and aircraft were actually fairly tardy in their switch to battle-readiness, and that German mines were laid with impunity, it becomes apparent that the Soviet Navy was but one step from a potential 'Pearl Harbor'.

Chapter 8

Far from the Front

The war was a serious trial for the Soviet State system, its structure of power and its endurance. There is no doubt: the onset of war came as a shock to the supreme leaders. Georgi Zhukov wrote in his memoirs:

> In the meantime, the first deputy Chief of staff, General Nikolai Vatoutin, reported that, after a heavy artillery bombardment, German land forces had advanced on the northwestern and western sectors. We immediately asked Stalin to organize a riposte and to deal counterblows on the enemy: 'Let's wait till Viacheslav Molotov's back,' he replied. Sometime later, Viacheslav Molotov entered the office: 'The German Government declared war on us.' Josef Stalin silently sunk into a chair and his own thoughts. A long, agonizing, pause set in . . .[1]

Numerous memoirs and researches have been dedicated to the actions and decision-making of the Soviet leadership during the first hours of the war. The price the country would have to pay in order to survive until the next day of peace – 9 May 1945 – was too high. Analysis and interpretation of documents and recollections of eyewitnesses is ongoing. However, as the wartime generation passes, the issue loses its poignancy and painfulness, shifting from journalism to history.

Nevertheless, within minutes, the men sitting in Stalin's room would take decisions and send directives. True, not always the right ones – originating from the false perceptions and information – but necessary for reorganization and setting the whole country on 'the rails of war'. The complicated and unpredictable character of the

first days of war plunged the Soviet Government into crisis, leading
to the establishment of new extraordinary bodies of power. Some
time was required to create the *Stavka* (Supreme Command – trans.)
and GKO (Gosudarstvennyi Komitet Oborony or State Defence
Committee – trans.), capable of steering the country through war.
But from the first hour of *Barbarossa*, no one sat idle, including the
Chairman of the Supreme Soviet of the USSR, Josef Stalin. That
day he decreed:

> 'On the mobilization of subjects to draft . . .'
> 'On the introduction of military law in some locations of the
> USSR . . .'
> 'On military law . . .'
> 'On the approval of regulations for military tribunals . . .'

From the above list, the mobilization issue stands out. The call-up
was announced across the whole country and affected all men born
between 1905 and 1918. Unlike other nations, the USSR initiated
full mobilization only after the first shots of war were fired. But, by
the end of July 1941, new armies would be formed to replace those
lost near the border, shocking the German Command out of its
euphoria following *Barbarossa*'s initial success.

Meanwhile, the editor-in-chief of the *Red Star* newspaper, David
Ortenberg, recalled:

> At about five in the morning, the *Narkom* returned from the
> Kremlin. I was summoned: 'The Germans have begun the
> war. Our trip to Minsk is cancelled. And you go to the *Red
> Star* [editor's office] and issue the newspaper . . .'
>
> Our old rotary press was printing the last thousands of the
> regular release of the *Red Star*, dated 22 June: quite a peace-
> time release, just routine army business – not a single word
> about the German-Fascist aggression. Even in the fourth
> section – almost fully dedicated to international events – the
> language was measured, emotionless. Now a sharp turn was
> needed! We would have to release a completely different
> newspaper.
>
> While I was trying to fathom where to start, the narrow
> corridors of the editorial office had already filled with people.

They stuffed the small conference-room with small suitcases, trench coats, and other travel paraphernalia. Everything was boiling up and buzzing in the editorial office. It was Sunday, the rest-day, but the bosses had come to work without being summoned. Everyone was in field gear, some even had compasses with them. Everyone was zealous to be there where the battle had already broken out.

After hot discussions on who would be going to which front, they came to see me with prepared applications. However, someone had to make the newspaper in Moscow, and someone would have to be held back in reserve in case unforeseen trips to the combat zone were needed. They couldn't accept this without resentment and squabbling: 'Why should I stay here – am I worse than the rest? Why such injustice?' I had to remind them that we observed military regulations and discipline . . .[2]

An hour after the meeting between Viacheslav Molotov and Schulenburg, the supreme Soviet leadership shifted into gear and the flywheel of actions contemplated by the mobilization plan began to turn. V.N. Novikov, Director of the Izhevsk mechanical plant, remembers:

> Early on the morning of 22 June 1941, having decided to have a bit of a rest, I went to the plant's lake to spend some time in the fresh air and do some fishing [. . .] We had just moved about 4km from the shore in a boat when we saw a cutter rushing towards us. Both the person on duty from the plant and the steersman were shouting: 'Vladimir Nikolaevich – it's war!'
>
> I went to the plant office in the clothes I'd taken for fishing. There I saw the First Secretary of the Oblast Party Committee, Alexei Chekinov, the Head of the Department of Internal Affairs, Mikhail Kouznetsov, and the director of the metallurgy works, Ivan Ostroushko. The secretaries of the City Party Committee, Fedor Kozlov and the District Party Committee, Grigory Sokolov, arrived almost the same time as me. The chief engineer and other senior functionaries of the plant were there too. Everyone was waiting for me because –

as director of the machine plant – I kept the mobilization plan we were meant to follow in case of war. The packet [with the plan] had been in the director's safe since the time when it used to be a united plant. I opened the packet [and found instructions] that the plant would have to increase production of rifles to 5,000 a day within a year. Production of sporting guns, motorcycles and some other goods for civilians would have to cease . . .[3]

Stalin categorically refused to broadcast an announcement – that was why Viacheslav Molotov assumed this important duty. The text of the announcement, which the whole population was to hear at 12.15, was prepared in the morning:

Men and women of the USSR! The Soviet Government and its head Comrade Stalin have entrusted me to make the following announcement:

Today, at four in the morning, without making any demands from the Soviet Union, without a declaration of war, German troops invaded our country, attacked our frontiers in many places, and bombed our cities – Zhitomir, Kiev, Sevastopol, Kaunas, and some others, killing and wounding more than two hundred people. Enemy air raids and artillery bombardment have also been undertaken from Romanian and the Finnish territories.

This attack on our country is a perfidy unparalleled in the history of civilized nations. The attack has been undertaken despite a non-aggression pact between the USSR and Germany, which the Soviet Government has been conscientiously observing. The attack has been undertaken despite the fact that – during the whole period of this agreement being in effect – the German Government has not been able to present the USSR with a single claim on the observation of the agreement. The German Fascist rulers are fully responsible for this predatory assault on the Soviet Union.

At 5.30 in the morning – after the attack had occurred – the German Ambassador in Moscow, Schulenburg, on behalf of his Government, informed me that the German Government had decided on war with the USSR, in light of a concentration of Red Army troops near the eastern border with Germany. In reply, it was declared on behalf of the Soviet Government that, till the last moment, the German Government had not presented the Soviet Government with any claims; that Germany had attacked the USSR despite the peaceful disposition of the Soviet Union and, thereby, Fascist Germany is the aggressor.

On the instructions of the Government of the Soviet Union, I have to declare that our troops and our aviation have committed no violation of the border at any place and, therefore, this morning's broadcast on Romanian radio, claiming attacks on Romanian aerodromes by Soviet aviation, is a complete lie and provocation. Today's declaration by Hitler – who is trying, post factum, to present a bill of particulars on the non-observation of the Soviet–German pact by the Soviet Union – is a similar piece of propaganda and provocation.

Only now – when the attack on the Soviet Union has already occurred – does the Soviet Government order our troops to repulse this predatory aggression and drive the German troops from our territory. This war has been imposed on us not by the German people, not by the German workers, peasants and intelligentsia, whose suffering is clearly comprehended by us, but the clique of bloodthirsty Fascist rulers who have enslaved the French, Czechs, Poles, Serbs, Norwegians, Belgians, Danes, Dutch, Greeks and [people's of] other nations.

The Government of the Soviet Union expresses the unshakeable confidence that our valiant Army and Navy, and the brave falcons of the Soviet Air Force, will do their duty before the Motherland, before the Soviet people, and will deal the aggressor a deadly blow. Now all our people will have to rally and unite as never before. Each of us has to demand from himself and from others discipline, orderliness, selflessness worthy of a real Soviet patriot, in order to [. . .] secure victory over the enemy.

Our people have to deal with an aggressive, jumped-up enemy, not for the first time. Once upon a time, our people responded to Napoleon's invasion of Russia with the Patriotic War, and Napoleon suffered a shattering defeat, precipitating his own collapse. The same will happen to the swaggering Hitler, who has declared a new crusade against our country. The Red Army and our whole nation will wage a new, victorious, patriotic war for the Motherland, for honour, for freedom [. . .] The Government urges you, citizens of the Soviet Union, to close ranks around our glorious Bolshevik Party, our Soviet Government, our great leader Comrade Stalin. Our cause is right. The enemy will be destroyed. The victory will be ours.[4]

Thus Viacheslav Molotov's speech ushered the war into every home. At midday, 22 June, the MKhAT [Moscow Arts Theatre – trans.] performed a regular play, *School for Scandal*. The spectators of this performance were among the very few who didn't hear Viacheslav Molotov's address. After the interval, a man in military uniform walked on stage and, having announced the outbreak of war, suggested that those subject to draft, head to their *voencomats* (military commissariats – trans.). All others remained in the auditorium and the performance was finished as usual. In the evening of 22 June, the men of the MKhAT made one more performance. No one could know that, several days later, German tanks would enter the streets of Minsk.

Even those related to troops of the near-border Districts were to hear of the outbreak of war from the radio broadcast at midday. A mechanic of the 94th Aviation Regiment (62nd Aviation Division, Kiev Military District), Ivan Eremievsky, remembered:

It was the month of June and I was on vacation. When leaving for my holiday, I bought a portable radio and took it to the village – I heard the declaration of war on that radio. At 12 a.m., Levitan [a famous Soviet radio broadcaster – trans.] began to broadcast news, and the first piece was that German troops in Africa had advanced. The minutes passed. At 12.12 he said that such-and-such a shaft in Donbass [Donetsk Coal

Basin – trans.] had fulfilled its plan. The radio fell silent [. . .]
Then, at 12.14, Levitan announced: 'Today, at 12.15 precisely,
the People's Commissar of Foreign Affairs, Comrade
Molotov, will deliver a speech. All radio stations of the Soviet
Union are on air.' Levitan repeated this several times [. . .] [At]
12.15 Viacheslav Molotov gave his speech . . .[5]

But those who lived close to the western border of the Soviet
Union didn't need a radio broadcast to learn about the war – they
heard it from screaming shells and shrieking dive-bombers. Ion
Degen remembers:

> On the night of 22 June, being a train driver on duty, I
> watched as a heavily laden train passed over the bridge to
> Germany. Early in the morning, people began to whisper:
> 'The war's begun!' Already, by daylight, our town had been
> bombed for the first time. Militiamen [i.e. policemen – trans.]
> shot at the German bombers with their revolvers – what a
> remarkable scene! [. . .] I ran to the town Komsomol
> committee, and from there to the voencomat, but no one
> wanted to talk to me. I rent the air with cries about a
> Komsomol member's duty, about defence of the Motherland,
> about the heroes of the Civil War. I repeated the slogans with
> which I'd been stuffed – like a dumpling with mashed potato.
> The answer was short: 'We don't draft kids into the army!'[6]

Petr Delyatitsky remembers the outbreak of the war in this way:

> My wife, Tatyana, born in 1929, was two years younger than
> me. Her father, Major Zinovy Ourin, was the commander of
> an artillery battalion in the 5th Army, and Tanya studied with
> me in the same school. At dawn on 22 June 1941, when the
> German airmen turned the military camp of Lutsk into a pile
> of smoking ruins, one of the bombs hit the house in which
> Tanya lived, and her mother and two younger brothers were
> trapped under the debris. Tanya rushed to the neighbours –
> Poles – and begged them to help dig her family out of the
> ruins. In reply, the Poles said: 'No way! No one invited you
> here, so you can kick the bucket!' [The Ukrainian town of

Lutsk had passed between Russia and Poland for hundreds of years, the population being mainly Polish and Jewish. In 1939 the town was annexed by the Soviet Union and many Poles arrested by the NKVD or deported into labour camps. The Germans finished off the Jewish population after the onset of *Barbarossa* – trans.]

On the night of 22 June I didn't go to bed. I sat in my room and read a book. Apparently I dozed off, and the book slipped out of my hands and fell on the floor. I reached for it and heard a noise. I glanced at my watch – it was 3.45 a.m. Again some strange sounds, similar to bursts of thunder, rang out. My Mum shouted to me: 'Pet'ka, shut the windows, the kids are scared by the storm.' I leaped to the window [. . .] The whole sky was black with aircraft. At that moment bombs began falling right in front of our house. They were falling on the tents of the commandant's platoon – soldiers were scampering out of there, dressed only in underpants and vests. Nearby were houses where the airmen lived. The airmen were dashing about and rushing headlong to the aerodrome of the I-16 fighters, situated behind an old Polish cemetery, not far from the Army HQ.

I stood as if spellbound, and couldn't take my eyes off this amazing and terrible scene. German planes flew so low that I saw with my own eyes as one of the pilots waved at me – a boy, standing at a lighted window. Do you understand? I saw it! After that I leaped out through the window, down to the street where Tamarin and the Kourenkov brothers were standing. We ran across the bog to fetch the machine-gun from the school, but the suspension bridge over the bog had already been destroyed. We rushed to the school down 17th Veresen Street, taking a shortcut through the old cemetery. But the bombing wouldn't stop. We had to remain in one of the crypts as the inferno raged all around. Not far from us, in one of the crypts, two strange men in civilian clothes were sitting and speaking into some apparatus. How could we comprehend, with our boyish minds, that those were German spotters with a two-way radio?

The raid was over and we ran into the woods, where the tankers from Mikhail Katoukov's division had always been stationed. We came across a well-dressed civilian, looking unlike a local Pole, walking towards us. He spoke to us in perfect Russian, with a grin: 'Boys, where are you running? Our troops are already in Germany, finishing off the *Nemets*!' [a common word for a German in Russian – trans.] [. . .] In the forest we encountered the tankers who were trying to start the engines of their machines, which had survived the air raid. We returned to the military camp again but our houses had already been destroyed. Everything was ablaze [. . .] Shops in the Chopin Street were burning nearby, cries for help were heard from one of them. We broke the door and pulled an old woman from the fire who had been staying overnight to safeguard the sausage shop. We returned to the DKS [officers' block – trans.] and couldn't understand anything: where were our families, did they manage to get out of the houses? Were they under the ruins?

And then another raid began. We rushed back to the forest, back to the unit from the 20th Tank Division. The tankers asked us: 'Boys, where are you from?' We replied: 'From the DKS, out of the military camp, we're children of officers, our homes have been bombed.' They seated us either on a tank or in a GAZ-3A vehicle and the column quit the forest.

On that day I discovered nothing about the fate of my kinfolk [. . .] We were in a brigade, retreating with heavy fighting from the Rovno–Lutsk area to Zhitomir [. . .] They dressed us up in old Red Army uniforms, gave us field caps, boots with puttees and old tarpaulin belts. Those were horrible days [. . .] It's enough just to remember it.[7]

For those who didn't find themselves under the deadly hand of the German war machine on 22 June, the day began normally. Yet that very day would come to symbolize the collapse of Hope: the hope of improving the quality of life; the hope of a quiet, rewarding job; the hope of successful studies; the hope of a good harvest. Yulia Drounina [a well-known Soviet poetess – trans.] remembered: 'Everyone's whole life had changed since that moment [. . .] and the question of one's tomorrow, one's place in this war arose before everyone.' And yet a facile optimism reigned over the country. The population was confident that the USSR was superior to Germany in military and technical matters. Grigory Sinyavsky, a prisoner who had been working on the construction of the Moscow–Minsk highway, recalls:

We were meant to have a day off on Sundays – and 22 June 1941 was no exception. Radio broadcasting was working at our plant and in the zone [a common Russian slang word for a penal labour colony – trans.]. On 22 June we heard Viacheslav Molotov's famous address and found out with the whole country that war had broken out. No one was scared by this news. Our mood was optimistic: 'Aha, you've got through? Well, you're gonna have your tail tweaked shortly!' We believed that the Germans would be smashed in several days. There was no sensation of war in Orsha on that day, although irregular armed battalions [similar to Home Guard in England – trans.] were organized in the city immediately. And we kept doing our time and working. The only thing that differed in our way of life was that we began digging slit trenches all over the city and introduced blackout in our location.[8]

And yet there were people who perceived the war indifferently. Mariana Milyutina remembers:

The war began when I was a third-year student of the 1st Institute of Medicine. On that day we had our exam on physiology, which I didn't know [well]. I studied with a lot of difficulties. And when I'd heard on the radio that the war had broken out, I thought: 'Good! Maybe, they will give me a mark '3' [i.e. third grade, meaning 'satisfactory' – trans.].' Indeed, the professor didn't care too much about anything and he was giving marks almost automatically. And so relief was my first feeling.[9]

And some even took the news with joy. A certain Olimpiada Polyakova wrote in her diary:

I can't believe that our liberation is coming. Whatever the Germans are, they're not going to be worse than this

[Bolshevik regime – trans]. And why should we care about the Germans? After all, we will live without them [it seems the author dreamed of an independent Russian state – trans.]. Everyone has such a feeling that 'here we are, at last it has come'; what we have been waiting for so long, what we couldn't even hope for [. . .] And there is no doubt that the Germans will win. God, forgive me! I'm not an enemy of my people, my Motherland [. . .] But we have to face the truth: all of us, the whole of Russia, are zealously wishing the enemy to win whatever he is. This accursed system [i.e. Communism – trans.] had stolen everything from us, including the feeling of patriotism.[10]

As suggested by the sentiments expressed above, some Soviet citizens hated Stalin's regime. As for Olimpiada Polyakova, she would find herself in German-occupied Krasnogvardeisk, near besieged Leningrad, struggling to survive the famine of the first winter of war. Much later, in spring 1945, Polyakova was found in a refugee camp near Munich by her acquaintance, Vera Pirozhkova:

Now she was mad at the Germans and declared that all of them should be locked in a concentration camp. I asked: 'All of them?' She thought for a second and then firmly replied: 'All of them!'[11]

Most of those who were to be called to the colours over the next four years (in other words, men born between 1919 and 1926) accepted Viacheslav Molotov's announcement as a matter of course – it was time to go and defend the Motherland. Yulia Drounina, recalls:

When war broke out I had no doubt, even for a minute, that the enemy would be smashed instantly [. . .] I was afraid that it would happen without my participation, that I wouldn't manage to get to the front.[12]

This mood was typical for the majority of young patriots educated by 'victorious' movies like *If War Comes Tomorrow*, the work of writers like Nikolai Shpanov and by massive State propaganda. The staff department of the Central Committee of the Bolshevik Party reported:

The mobilization is conducted in an organized manner, according to the intended plan. The draftees' mood is sprightly and confident [. . .] Many applications to join the Red Army arrive [. . .] There are many cases where girls request to be sent to the front [. . .] meetings at factories and plants, in *kolkhozes* [i.e. State farms – trans] and institutions are conducted with a sharp increase in patriotism.[13]

Unlike the young people – who were treating the current events almost as a festivity – the older generation, which remembered the First World War, felt no euphoria and prepared for the long-standing deprivations to come. Queues grew quickly at shops and markets during the very first hours of the war. People were buying up salt, matchsticks, soap, sugar and other living essentials. Many people were taking their savings from banks and trying to cash Government bonds. Generally speaking, the mood was optimistic – few defeatist sentiments were observed. Samples from a few testimonies of those who witnessed these cataclysmic events and survived follow.

Lev Poushkarev:

I was preparing for my third-year exams in the Pedagogic Institute, studying in the Lenin Library. Usually, by 9 or 10 a.m., all seats were occupied, and there were queues. But that Sunday [22 June – ed.] the room was deserted for unknown reasons. And when we went to receive our books we got a shock: 'War has begun.' We went outside and witnessed a deserted Moscow. Everyone had rushed to the shops to buy necessities – salt, matchsticks and so on. We were told that, since we were third-year students, we would have to finish our course and pass our exams. And so we passed the exams in late June [but] I have to say that no one cared too much about them. During the first days of July we volunteered to dig trenches.[14]

Dmitri Boulgakov:

I lived in the village of Skorodnoye, [in the] Bolshesoldatsky District of the Kursk Oblast. The fate of this village was tragic [. . .] On that day, 22 June, it was raining hard. I was at home. Suddenly, I saw my friend Serezha run across the mud. The Finnish War [1939–1940] had ended without us and we assumed we'd never get a chance to be soldiers [. . .] Serezha was running: 'War!' We ran to the [village] club across the mud. People were gathering there. There were no regional officials, only local activists – the book-keeper, the accountant. They were making public speeches: 'We'll smash them!' [. . .] And in a few months, when the Germans had come around, they would collect eggs for them [. . .] We felt sorrow that we wouldn't participate in the war: the Germans would be smashed quickly and we'd have no share again . . .[15]

Nikolai Doupak:

In June 1941 I was nineteen years of age. I was acting in Dovzhenko's [a famous Soviet film director – trans.] *Taras Boul'ba* movie as Andrei. On Saturday and Sunday we had days off and spent them in Kiev. We were told we would have to watch some foreign movie, and to do that we would have to be in the studio on Sunday at 12 a.m. I was reading and re-reading something on Saturday, so I went to bed late and woke up to the sound of shooting. I went out onto the balcony – a man came out from the adjacent room: 'What's that?' – 'Maybe manoeuvres of the Kiev Military District.' As soon as he spoke, an aircraft – about 100m away and marked with a Swastika – bombed a bridge across the Dnieper. It was at about five in the morning [. . .] The neighbour grew pale – this wasn't like manoeuvres at all. We walked down. No one knew anything. No one came to pick me up. I went to the studio by tram. Then, suddenly, there was another air raid. They dropped a bomb on the Jewish bazaar – the first casualties. I arrived at the studio and heard Viacheslav Molotov's address. The picture became clear. Alexander Dovshenko came out and said that, within a year, we would be smashing the enemy on his territory. Such was the mood. But next day, when we arrived for filming, the crowd scene in which soldiers were supposed to participate had been cancelled. Then we understood that, sorry, this is serious and will last a long time.[16]

Tamara Ivanova:

I was ten years of age when the war begun. We lived in Anapa, in Nizhegorodskaya Street. It was Sunday. I went to the movies with my girlfriends. The 'Spartak' movie theatre was situated in the 'Blue Wave' sanatorium. Before the show I walked down to the sea and found a pistol in a boat. I thought it was a toy, took it, but it turned out to be heavy. I was scared and threw it into the water. It was like a sign [. . .] Why had I come across this pistol? I shouted to my girlfriends. We tried to get it back – the water was clear, calm, but we failed. We returned to the movie theatre and they announced that war had begun. I ran home. My father already knew about the war – they'd bombed Kiev, Sevastopol [. . .] I told him: 'I wish one bomb would fall on us, so we could see what it looks like.' He said: 'If you want to see one, have a look at the shell.' In our yard there was a Turkish shell. Half of it was in the ground but the bottom stuck out. I used to crack nuts on it. Then he walked me to the museum in Pushkin Street. There we looked at round shells and bombs. I don't remember what they were made of. He showed me all that and said that it was very scary.[17]

Nikolai Ovsyannikov:

The war began very routinely. Not like I see it in the movies. Maybe it was like that somewhere but not at our place. Me and my mates swam at a beach on 22 June, then we walked home. It was 2 p.m. The city broadcasting centre – a one-storey building on a high plinth – used to be where the Veterans' Council is now. What's happening?! About forty or fifty men stood near the centre window, someone put a loudspeaker on the window sill. Someone makes some kind of speech. We stopped, asked what was happening: 'The war has begun! Viacheslav Molotov makes an announcement.' And we heard only the end of his speech. Thus, for the first time, I heard about the war. We rushed to the *OSAVIAKhIM* [Abbreviation for the 'Society of Assistance to the Aviation and Chemical Defence' – trans.] straightaway. The head of the *OSAVIAKhIM* was making phone calls and there was such a hustle and bustle. He said: 'Guys, come with me to the City Council.' We went and walked up to the first floor – there was the chief, who said: 'We have to announce to the city population that the war has begun.' This may seem strange now, but that's how life was back then. I lived with my family in Kirov Street. There were only two radio loud-speakers in the whole block – one in my house and another in a neighbour's, three or four courts away from us. It was not surprising, therefore, that he said it was necessary to inform the population about the war. He opened a side-curtain, behind which was a map of the city. He assigned a street to each of us: 'Go and announce that the war has begun.' I went with my mate, Fedya Kravchenko. We entered an empty court and yelled: 'Master!' – 'What do you want?' – 'Come here. Have you heard that the war has begun . . ?' – 'No.' – '. . . Against Germany. We've been charged with letting everyone, including you, know that you have to observe black-out. All windows need to be curtained at night so that no light is seen.' – 'What for?!' We explained: to prevent bombing. And so we passed through several blocks in the same way . . .[18]

Sophia Fatkoulina:

When the war began – that was such a terrible scene! Horsemen kept riding about, announcing that fighting had broken out. The men of call-up age went to the *voencomat* – I remember a lot of men going there. Then there was the scene on the banks of the Volga – men heading off to the front on steamships. You know, everyone stood on the bank and the whole Volga was in tears . . .[19]

Grigory Shishkin:

I was born in 1924 in Moscow. In the summer of 1941 I went on holiday to a village in the Voronezh Oblast, where my grandparents lived. I heard the announcement on the beginning of the war when I was walking with mother and grandmother to the shop, which was in the middle of the village. I always walked there with them, for there was a horizontal gymnastics bar near the shop, on which I trained while they were shopping. Back then it was a custom among the youths to brag who could do more pull-ups, run faster, swim farther [. . .] The heat was horrible! Everything seemed desolate – no sound, nothing, such was the calm. And suddenly we heard Viacheslav Molotov's speech, announcing the war from loud-speakers fixed on poles. Howling broke out, the village womenfolk were in tears, the dogs began to bark and howl – a great bustle began straightaway. This noise stayed in my memory [. . .] I thought: 'Why are they crying, one has to rejoice? We'll smash the Fascists quickly!' That was the way we'd been taught. We, schoolchildren, immediately ran to the *voencomat*. The *voencom* [military commissar – trans.] says: 'You're too early, guys, you have to finish ten years at school.[20]

Igor Samoroukov:

And when suddenly, on 22 June, several minutes before midday, it sounded on the radio that Molotov's speech was coming, my heart missed a beat. I understood that Germany had attacked. Then me and other boys ran out into the street. Powerful loud-speakers were out there and people were already gathering. Everyone held his breath, waiting what Viacheslav Molotov was going to say. So, Molotov began his speech. He said something like: 'Today at four in the morning the German Army crossed the border over the whole front from the Baltic to the Black Sea and advanced . . .'. It was Sunday, many people were going to the countryside. Back then, people had no *dachas*, and on Sundays everyone would go to the country with a lot of gear and hammocks. The whole crowd moving towards Kolkhoznaya Square stopped to listen to Viacheslav Molotov. At first there was total silence. Literally, one could hear a fly humming. And suddenly a female yell resounded: 'What kind of idiots we are, what fools! There's been nothing we wouldn't send to the Germans! I myself live next to a train station, there are trains full of grain heading to Germany one after the other. We've clothed them up, shoed them up, fed them up. What fools we are! Who have we been feeding . . .?!' And she burst into tears.

When I returned to my yard, many women were crying there too, because all of them had sons of call-up age or already in the Army. But by evening, life was going on as if nothing had happened. Some people even went to the countryside, but the majority stayed at home. Unfamiliar young men appeared in our court and began to say that we would have to dig an earth shelter. We couldn't imagine that bombing would be possible – after all, Smolensk seemed so far from the front. The strangers simply said that German air raids were possible. Our gunners would have to shoot at them, and splinters from our flak shells might hit civilians, so to prevent this we had to dig shelters. The young men explained how to do it. But I'll tell you that, when I found myself in the Army two-and-a-half years later, and they began to teach us how to dig trenches, I remembered the trench in our court and concluded that it would have been good only as a common grave! But I've run a few steps forward here. It was still the peaceful 22 June. And only on the next day did German planes fly over Smolensk . . .[21]

Alexei Maximenko:

I met with the war in Kuibyshev, on my way to the place of service. The train stopped. I walked out onto the platform, took a mug of beer, then watched as people gathered around a loud-speaker: 'War!' Women were crossing themselves. I didn't finish my mug of beer and got back on the train so as not to miss it. I seated myself in the carriage and everyone spoke only about the war: 'How come?! We've got the treaty of friendship with the Germans?! Why have they started it?!' Someone older says: 'Certainly, they promised [peace], but look – they've already captured half of Europe, now it's our turn. There were bourgeois states, they occupied them, but we have a Communist regime – it's like a fishbone in the throat for them. Now it's gonna be hard for us to fight them.' I understood that something terrible had happened, but back then, being eighteen years of age, I failed to assess the whole tragic nature and complexity of the situation . . .[22]

Valentin Rychkov:

I lived in Kiselevsk, Kemerovo Oblast. People's reaction to the outbreak of war varied. Adults faced the war with tears in their eyes, exchanged opinions, understood that a terrible calamity was coming. But we youngsters [faced it] with enthusiasm. We gathered in the city gardens at the dance pavilion. We split into two groups. One group of 'military specialists' was asserting that in two or three weeks nothing would be left of the Fascists. The second – the more sedate one – was saying: 'No, not two or three weeks but two or three months, and it will be our complete victory – the Fascists will be destroyed.' An unusual phenomenon was adding fervour to this. At that time the sunset in the west was not typical but blood-red! Some were saying: 'This is our Red Army – it has struck the Germans so hard, with all its firepower, that we can see it even in Siberia!' But it was a utopia, of course. As of me, I stood with my thoughts. My friend Romashko asked me: 'And you, Val'ka, why are you standing quiet and not giving your opinion?' And I said: 'No, guys, to achieve victory will take no less than two or three years.' What a commotion broke out! There was no curse I didn't hear! How badly they accused me! I thought they would break my nose! I can't explain why, but I was sure that it would be nothing like two or three weeks, and so I said 'two or three years'. As it turned out, I was nearer the truth, but still badly mistaken . . .[23]

Conclusion

Every Soviet citizen alive at that time remembered the first day of *Barbarossa* – it became a borderline, dividing life into 'before' and 'after'. But from a military viewpoint, it was not so significant: the decisions made on that day did not radically change the situation. The timely withdrawal of the 6th and the 42nd Rifle Divisions from the Brest Citadel might have preserved them a little longer as cohesive combat units; but it would be naïve to believe they could have held the 2nd Panzer Group. The turning point was actually passed before the invasion, when the chance to deploy the Red Army near the western border was missed, thereby sealing the fate of the covering armies. Due to tardy deployment, the Soviet Command could only oppose the three German Army Groups with a rarefied screen of individual regiments and battalions. This Soviet force was fit for one purpose only: to contain minor border incidents. Furthermore, 22 June was not the bloodiest day in the history of *Barbarossa*, and it would be a mistake to reckon that, having achieved the strategic initiative, the Germans immediately destroyed the Red Army. As Hitler allegedly expressed it: 'On 22 June we smashed the door open without realising what was behind it.'[1]

As for Stalin, he did not directly address the Soviet public until 3 July 1941 – nearly two weeks after *Barbarossa* began:

> Comrades! Citizens! Brothers and sisters! Soldiers! I am addressing you, my friends!
>
> What is required to eliminate the danger hanging over our country? What measures must be taken to defeat the enemy?
>
> First, it is necessary that the Soviet people understand the depth of the danger that threatens our country and abandon all complacency [. . .] The enemy is cruel and pitiless. He aims to seize our lands, watered with our sweat, to seize our grain and oil, secured by our labour. He aims to restore the

rule of the landlords [and] to destroy the national culture and statehood of [. . .] the Soviet Union . . .[2]

Despite the delayed delivery, Stalin had a point: Nazi policy was to view the Slavic peoples as sub-humans fit only for slaughter or slavery. For ordinary Soviet citizens, then, *Barbarossa* was a battle for survival; and though the Soviet Union would eventually prevail, some 27 million of its citizens would perish.

One Red Army volunteer who left for the front in 1941 was playwright, journalist and poet Konstantin Simonov. One the eve of his leaving he wrote a poem entitled 'Wait for Me', which successfully caught the heartbeat of the nation, while anticipating the horrors to come – the long road back to peace.

Wait for me and I'll come back,
Dodging every fate!
'What a piece of luck!' they'll say,
Those who would not wait.
They will never understand
How amidst the strife,
By your waiting for me, dear,
You had saved my life.
Only you and I will know
How you got me through.
Simply – you knew how to wait –
No one else but you.[3]

Order of Battle

GERMAN FORCES

<u>Army Group North (Wilhelm Ritter von Leeb)</u>
Sixteenth Army (Ernst Busch)
4th Panzer Group (Erich Hoepner)
18th Army (Georg von Küchler)
Air Fleet 1 (Alfred Keller)

*

Stationed in East Prussia with twenty-six divisions.
Army Group Centre (Fedor von Bock)
Fourth Army (Günther von Kluge)
2nd Panzer Group (Heinz Guderian)
3rd Panzer Group (Hermann Hoth)
Ninth Army (Adolf Strauss)
Air Fleet 2 (Albert Kesselring)

*

Stationed in Eastern Poland with forty-nine divisions.
Army Group South (Gerd von Rundstedt)
Seventeenth Army (Carl-Heinrich von Stülpnagel)
1st Panzer Group (Ewald von Kleist)
Eleventh Army (Eugen Ritter von Schobert)
Sixth Army (Walther von Reichenau)
Air Fleet 4 (Alexander Löhr)

*

Stationed in Southern Poland and Romania with forty-one divisions, including Slovak, Hungarian and Romanian troops.
Army High Command Norway (Nikolaus von Falkenhorst)
Stationed in Norway with two corps of infantry plus air support from Air Fleet 5.

SOVIET FORCES

Note: 'Fortified District' units were attached to local Front or Army command. Tasked with manning pillboxes on the border, each unit consisted of approximately 3,000 troops.

<u>Leningrad Military District (Northern Front) (Lieutenant General M.M. Popov)</u>
Attached to Front HQ
177th Rifle Division
191st Rifle Division
8th Rifle Brigade
21st, 22nd, 25th, 29th Fortified District

*

7th Army (Lieutenant General F.D. Gorelenko)
54th Rifle Division
71st Rifle Division
168th Rifle Division
237th Rifle Division
26th Fortified District

*

14th Army (Lieutenant General V.A. Frolov)
42nd Rifle Corps
 - 104th Rifle Division
 - 122nd Rifle Division
14th Rifle Division
52nd Rifle Division
23rd Fortified District

*

23rd Army (Major General P.S. Pshennikov)
19th Rifle Corps
 - 115th Rifle Division
 - 142nd Rifle Division

50th Rifle Corps
- 43rd Rifle Division
- 70th Rifle Division
- 123rd Rifle Division
27th and 28th Fortified District
10th Mechanized Corps
- 21st Tank Division
- 24th Tank Division
- 198th Motorized Division
- 7th Motorcycle Regiment
1st Mechanized Corps
- 1st Tank Division
- 3rd Tank Division
- 163rd Motorized Division

Baltic Special Military District
   (Northwestern Front) (Colonel
   General F.I. Kouznetsov)
Attached to Front HQ
65th Rifle Corps (Headquarters)
41st Fortified District
5th Airborne Corps
- 9th Airborne Brigade
- 10th Airborne Brigade
- 201st Airborne Brigade

*

8th Army (Lieutenant General P.P.
   Sobennikov)
10th Rifle Corps
- 10th Rifle Division
- 48th Rifle Division
- 90th Rifle Division
11th Rifle Corps
- 11th Rifle Division
- 125th Rifle Division
44th, 48th Fortified District
12th Mechanized Corps
- 23rd Tank Division
- 28th Tank Division
- 202nd Motorized Division
- 10th Motorcycle Regiment

*

11th Army (Lieutenant General V.I.
   Morozov)

- 23rd Rifle Division
- 126th Rifle Division
- 128th Rifle Division
16th Rifle Corps
- 5th Rifle Division
- 33rd Rifle Division
- 188th Rifle Division
29th Rifle Corps
- 179th Rifle Division
- 181st Rifle Division
42nd, 45th, 46th Fortified District
3rd Mechanized Corps
- 2nd Tank Division
- 5th Tank Division
- 84th Motorized Division

*

27th Army (Major General M.E.
   Berzarin)
- 16th Rifle Division
- 67th Rifle Division
- 3rd Rifle Brigade
22nd Rifle Corps
- 180th Rifle Division
- 183rd Rifle Division
24th Rifle Corps
- 181st Rifle Division
- 183rd Rifle Division

Western Special Military District
   (Western Front) (Colonel
   General D.G. Pavlov)
Attached to Front HQ
58th, 61st, 63rd, 64th, 65th Fortified
   Districts
13th Army (Headquarters only)
2nd Rifle Corps
- 100th Rifle Division
- 161st Rifle Division
21st Rifle Corps
- 17th Rifle Division
- 24th Rifle Division
- 37th Rifle Division
44th Rifle Corps
- 64th Rifle Division
- 108th Rifle Division

47th Rifle Corps
- 50th Rifle Division
- 55th Rifle Division
- 121st Rifle Division
- 143rd Rifle Division
4th Airborne Corps
- 7th Airborne Brigade
- 8th Airborne Brigade
- 214th Airborne Brigade
- 8th Antitank Brigade
17th Mechanized Corps
- 27th Tank Division
- 36th Tank Division
- 209th Motorized Division
- 22nd Motorcycle Regiment
20th Mechanized Corps
- 26th Tank Division
- 38th Tank Division
- 210th Motorized Division
- 24th Motorcycle Regiment

*

*3rd Army (Lieutenant General V.I.
   Kouznetsov)*
4th Rifle Corps
- 27th Rifle Division
- 56th Rifle Division
- 85th Rifle Division
68th Fortified District
11th Mechanized Corps
- 29th Tank Division
- 33rd Tank Division
- 204th Motorized Division
- 7th Antitank Brigade
- 16th Motorcycle Regiment

*

*4th Army (Lieutenant General A.A.
   Korobkov)*
28th Rifle Corps
- 6th Rifle Division
- 42nd Rifle Division
- 49th Rifle Division
- 75th Rifle Division
62nd Fortified District
14th Mechanized Corps

- 22nd Tank Division
- 30th Tank Division
- 205th Motorized Division
- 20th Motorcycle Regiment

*

*10th Army (Major General K.D.
   Goloubev)*
1st Rifle Corps
- 2nd Rifle Division
- 8th Rifle Division
5th Rifle Corps
- 13th Rifle Division
- 85th Rifle Division
- 113th Rifle Division
6th Cavalry Corps
- 6th Cavalry Division
- 36th Cavalry Division
- 155th Rifle Division
66th Fortified District
6th Mechanized Corps
- 4th Tank Division
- 7th Tank Division
- 29th Mechanized Division
- 4th Motorcycle Regiment
13th Mechanized Corps
- 25th Tank Division
- 31st Tank Division
- 208th Mechanized Division
- 18th Motorcycle Regiment

*

Kiev Special Military District
   (Southwestern Front)
   (Lieutenant General M.P.
   Kirponos)
Attached to Front HQ
31st Rifle Corps
- 193rd Rifle Division
- 195th Rifle Division
- 200th Rifle Division
36th Rifle Corps
- 140th Rifle Division
- 146th Rifle Division
- 228th Rifle Division
49th Rifle Corps

- 190th Rifle Division
- 197th Rifle Division
- 199th Rifle Division
55th Rifle Corps
- 130th Rifle Division
- 169th Rifle Division
- 189th Rifle Division
1st Airborne Corps
- 1st Airborne Brigade
- 204th Airborne Brigade
- 211th Airborne Brigade
1st, 3rd, 5th, 7th, 13th, 15th, 17th
  Fortified District
19th Mechanized Corps
- 40th Tank Division
- 43rd Tank Division
- 213th Motorized Division
24th Mechanized Corps
- 45th Tank Division
- 49th Tank Division
- 216th Motorized Division

*

*5th Army (Major General M.I.
  Potapov)*
15th Rifle Corps
- 45th Rifle Division
- 62nd Rifle Division
27th Rifle Corps
- 87th Rifle Division
- 124th Rifle Division
- 135th Rifle Division
2nd Fortified District
9th Mechanized Corps
- 20th Tank Division
- 35th Tank Division
- 131st Motorized Division
22nd Mechanized Corps
- 19th Tank Division
- 41st Tank Division
- 215th Motorized Division

*

*6th Army (Lieutenant General I.N.
  Mouzychenko)*
6th Rifle Corps

- 41st Rifle Division
- 97th Rifle Division
- 159th Rifle Division
37th Rifle Corps
- 80th Rifle Division
- 139th Rifle Division
- 141st Rifle Division
4th, 6th Fortified District
4th Mechanized Corps
- 8th Tank Division
- 32nd Tank Division
- 81st Motorized Division
15th Mechanized Corps
- 10th Tank Division
- 37th Tank Division
- 212th Motorized Division
5th Cavalry Corps
- 3rd Cavalry Division
- 14th Cavalry Division

*

*12th Army (Major General P.G.
  Ponedelin)*
13th Rifle Corps
- 44th Rifle Division
- 58th Rifle Division
- 192nd Mountain Rifle Division
17th Rifle Corps
- 60th Rifle Division
- 96th Mountain Rifle Division
- 164th Rifle Division
10th, 11th, 12th Fortified District
16th Mechanized Corps
- 15th Tank Division
- 39th Tank Division
- 240th Motorized Division

*

*26th Army (Lieutenant General F. Ya
  Kostenko)*
8th Rifle Corps
- 99th Rifle Division
- 173rd Rifle Division
- 72nd Mountain Rifle Division
8th Fortified District
8th Mechanized Corps

- 34th Tank Division
- 7th Motorized Division

*

9th Independent Army (Odessa
   Military District) (Lieutenant
   General Ya. T. Cherevichenko)
Attached to Army HQ
14th Rifle Corps
- 25th Rifle Division
- 51st Rifle Division
35th Rifle Corps
- 95th Rifle Division
- 176th Rifle Division
48th Rifle Corps
- 30th Mountain Rifle Division
- 74th Rifle Division
- 150th Rifle Division
2nd Mechanized Corps
- 11th Tank Division
- 16th Tank Division
- 15th Motorized Division
2nd Cavalry Corps
- 11th Cavalry Division
- 16th Cavalry Division
18th Mechanized Corps
- 44th Tank Division
- 47th Tank Division
- 218th Motorized Division

*

Soviet Air Force Units
Northern Air Force (Northern Front)
(Major General Protsevetkin)
3rd Fighter Aviation Division
39th Fighter Aviation Division
54th Fighter Aviation Division
1st Mixed Aviation Division
2nd Mixed Aviation Division

55th Mixed Aviation Division
5th Mixed Aviation Division
41st Bomber Aviation Division

*

Baltic Special Military District Air
Force (Northwestern Front) (Major
General A. Ionov)
57th Fighter Aviation Division
4th Mixed Aviation Division
6th Mixed Aviation Division
7th Mixed Aviation Division
8th Mixed Aviation Division

*

Kiev Special Military District Air
Force (Southwestern Front) (Major
General A. Ionov)
19th Bomber Aviation Division
62nd Bomber Aviation Division
44th Fighter Aviation Division
64th Fighter Aviation Division
14th Mixed Aviation Division
15th Mixed Aviation Division
16th Mixed Aviation Division
17th Mixed Aviation Division
63rd Mixed Aviation Division

Odessa Military District Air Force
(Supporting 9th Independent Army)
(General F.G. Mishugin)
20th Mixed Aviation Division
21st Mixed Aviation Division
45th Mixed Aviation Division

Black Sea Air Force (Supporting the
Black Sea Fleet)
62nd Fighter Brigade
63rd Bomber Brigade

Sources

Preface
1. Das Memorandum: wie der Sowjetunion der Krieg erklärt wurde, 1981.
2. V.M. Berezhkov, *Pages of Diplomatic History*, Moscow International Affairs, 1987.
3. G. Hilger, *Wir und Kreml*, Frankfurt, 1956.

Chapter 1
1. Generaloberst F. Halder, *Kriegstagebuch: Tagliche Aufzeichnungen des Chefs des Generalstabes des Heeres 1939–1942*, Bd. 2, Von der geplanten Landung in England bis zum Beginn des Ostfeldzuges, Stuttgart, W. Kohlhammer Vl, 1963.
2. Hubatsch Walther, *Hitler's Weisungen für die Kriegführung 1939–1945*, Frankfurt a/M., 1962.
3. A. Drabkin, *Penetrating Enemy Lines: Stories of Scouts*, Moscow, Yauza, 2010.
4. H. Wehner, *Zeugnis*, Koln, 1988.
5. Lev Maidanik, interview with Artem Drabkin, http://www.iremember.ru/.
6. N. Obryn'ba, *Red Partisan*, Barnsley, 2006.
7. Mikhail Sandler, interview with Artem Drabkin, http://www.iremember.ru/.
8. Rostislav Zhidkov, interview with Artem Drabkin, http://www.iremember.ru/.
9. Dmitri Boulgakov, interview with Artem Drabkin, http://www.iremember.ru/.
10. Alexsander Bourtsev, interview with Artem Drabkin, http://www.iremember.ru/.
11. Viktor Sinaisky, interview with Artem Drabkin, http://www.iremember.ru/.
12. Mikhail Sandler, interview with Artem Drabkin, http://www.iremember.ru/.
13. A. Drabkin, *Barbarossa and the Retreat to Moscow*, Barnsley, 2007.
14. N.V. Avvakumov, *First Salvoes of War*, Sverdlovsk Middle Ural publisher, 1991.
15. I. Kh. Bagramyan, *This Way War Began*, Moscow, Voenizdat, 1971.
16. S.A. Gladysh and V.I. Milovanov, *Eighth Army: Operational Record During the Great Patriotic War*, Moscow War History Institution, 1994.
17. Ivan Garshtya, interview with Artem Drabkin, http://www.iremember.ru/.

18. Mikhail Badanes, interview with Artem Drabkin, http://www.iremember.ru/.
19. Rostislav Zhidkov, interview with Artem Drabkin, http://www.iremember.ru/.
20. Petr Delyatitsky, interview with Artem Drabkin, http://www.iremember.ru/.
21. A. Drabkin, *I fought on Il-2*, Moscow Eksmo, 2005.
22. Vladimir Vinogradov, interview with Artem Drabkin, http://www.iremember.ru/.
23. Olga Khod'ko, interview with Artem Drabkin, http://www.iremember.ru/.
24. M. Zakharov, *General Staff Before the War*, Moscow, AST, 2005.
25. A. Yakovlev, *1941, Documents*, Volume 2, *Moscow Democracy*, 1998.
26. Ibid.
27. *Pravda*, 14 June 1941.
28. Anatoly Khonyak, interview with Artem Drabkin, http://www.iremember.ru/.

Chapter 2
1. *Military History Journal*, Moscow No. 9, 1960.
2. Ibid.
3. Alexander Panuev, interview with Artem Drabkin, http://www.iremember.ru/.
4. *Military History Journal*, Moscow No. 5, 1989.
5. S.S. Matsapoura, *Comrade Sergeant*, Moscow Voenizdat, 1976.
6. Paul Carell, *Hitler Moves East, 1941–1943*, New York, 1964.
7. N.I. Afanasiev, *Front Without Rear: Notes of a Partisan Commander*, Leningrad, Lenizdat, 1983.
8. Daniil Zlatkin, interview with Artem Drabkin, http://www.iremember.ru/.
9. Semen Danich, interview with Artem Drabkin, http://www.iremember.ru/.
10. I.L. Drouyan, *We Hold our Oath*, Minsk, 1975.
11. Alexander Kopanev, interview with Artem Drabkin, http://www.iremember.ru/.
12. S.S. Vorkov, *Miles of Courage*, Kiev Politizdat, 1987.
13. I.N. Roussyanov, *Born in Battles*, Moscow, Voenizdat, 1982.
14. Valentina Vorob'eva, interview with Artem Drabkin, http://www.iremember.ru/.
15. *USSR State Security Bodies During the Great Patriotic War*, Volume 2, *Outbreak*, Book 1, Moscow 2003.
16. G.K. Zhukov, *Memoirs and Reflections*, Moscow Olma-Press 2002.
17. A. Yakovlev, *1941, Documents*, Volume 2, *Moscow Democracy*, 1998.

Chapter 3
1. Vladimir Osaulenko, interview with Artem Drabkin, http://www.iremember.ru/.
2. Nakhman Doushansky, interview with Artem Drabkin, http://www.iremember.ru/.
3. P.A. Rotmistrov, *Steel Guard Moscow*, Voenizdat, 1984.
4. *The Initial Period of War on the Eastern Front, 22 June–August 1941: Proceedings of the Fourth Art of War Symposium*, ed. by Colonel David M. Glantz, Frank Cass series on Soviet military experience, Volume 2, London, 2001, p. 112.
5. E. Raus, *Panzer Operations: the Eastern Front Memoirs of General Raus, 1941–1945*, Da Capo Press, 2005.
6. Field Marshal Erich von Manstein, *Lost Victories*, Moscow Voenizdat, 1957.
7. G. Hoth, *Tank Operations*, Moscow Voenizdat, 1961.
8. Ibid.
9. S.S. Matsapoura, *Comrade Sergeant*, Moscow Voenizdat, 1976.
10. *Collection of War Documents No. 34*, Moscow, 1953.
11. Lazar Belkin, interview with Artem Drabkin, http://www.iremember.ru/.
12. A.A. Krupennikov, *In First Battles*, Collection of Articles, Krasnogorsk, 1998.
13. Ibid.
14. D. Egorov, *June 1941: West Front Annihilation*, Moscow Yauza, 2007.

Chapter 4
1. L.M. Sandalov, *Bypass*, Moscow Voenizdat, 1961.
2. L.M. Sandalov, *First Days of War*, Moscow Voenizdat, 1989.
3. R. Aliev, *Storm of Brest Fortress*, Moscow Eksmo, 2009.
4. Ibid.
5. Vladimir Osaulenko, interview with Artem Drabkin, http://www.iremember.ru/.
6. *Bug on Fire: Collection of Articles*, Minsk, 1965.
7. K.V. Malygin, *In the Centre of Battle Order*, Moscow Voenizdat, 1986.
8. Mikhail Sandler, interview with Artem Drabkin, http://www.iremember.ru/.

Chapter 5
1. Anatoly Loginov, interview with Artem Drabkin, http://www.iremember.ru/.
2. A. Kazakov, *On That War*, Moscow Zvezda No. 5, 2005.
3. *War Diary of Army Group South, Collection of Captured Documents Translations*, Institute of Military History, Ministry of Defence, 1968.
4. A.V. Egorov, *With Belief in Victory*, Moscow Voenizdat, 1974.
5. D.I. Ryabyshev, *First Year of War*, Moscow Voenizdat, 1990.
6. *Military History Journal*, No. 6, 1973.

7. Yuly Routman, interview with Artem Drabkin,
http://www.iremember.ru/.
8. *War Diary of Army Group South, Collection of Captured Documents Translations*, Institute of Military History, Ministry of Defence, 1968.
9. K.N. Galitsky, *Years of Rough Ordeals 1941–1944: Notes of an Army Commander*, Moscow Nauka, 1973.
10. Ibid.
11. Ibid.

Chapter 6
1. *Russian Archive Great Patriotic V 12(1–2), Documents of Conferences of RKKA High Command, 23–31 December 1940*, Moscow Terra, 1993.
2. Ibid.
3. Ibid.
4. Ibid.
5. A. Drabkin, *Barbarossa and the Retreat to Moscow*, Barnsley, 2007.
6. C. Bergstrom and A. Mikhailov, *Black Cross Red Star: the Air War Over the Eastern Front*, Volume 1, 2000.
7. W. Schwabedissen, *The Russian Air Force in the Eyes of German Commanders*, New York, 1960, pp. 90–91.
8. A. Drabkin, *Barbarossa and the Retreat to Moscow*, Barnsley, 2007.
9. *Collection of War Documents No. 34*, Moscow, 1953.
10. V. Efremov and N. Ilin, *Guards in the Air*, Moscow Yauza, 2006.
11. V. Olimpiev, *War View from the Trench*, Minsk, 2003.
12. D.B. Khazanov, *1941: Bitter Lessons: the War in the Air*, Moscow Eksmo, 2006.
13. Sergei Dolgoushin, interview with Artem Drabkin,
http://www.iremember.ru/.
14. N. Shpanov, *The First Blow: A Novel of Future War*, Moscow, 1939.
15. Ibid.
16. TSAMo RF, f.208, op. 2511, d.206, l.20.
17. A. Drabkin, *I Fought on a Fighter Plane*, Moscow Yauza, 2006.
18. N.S. Skripko, *On Targets Close and Distant*, Moscow Voenizdat, 1981.
19. Viktor Sinaisky, interview with Artem Drabkin,
http://www.iremember.ru/.
20. A.A. Krupennikov, *In First Battles*, Collection of Articles, Krasnogorsk, 1998.
21. Ibid.
22. D.B. Khazanov, *1941: Bitter Lessons: the War in the Air*, Moscow Eksmo, 2006.
23. Ibid.
24. Ibid.
25. Alexander Pavlichenko, interview with Artem Drabkin,
http://www.iremember.ru/.

26. N.G. Bogdanov, *Guards Gatchina's Regiment in the Air*, Leningrad Lenizdat, 1980.
27. N.S. Skripko, *On Targets Close and Distant*, Moscow Voenizdat, 1981.
28. Ibid.

Chapter 7
1. N. Kouznetsov, *On the Eve*, Moscow Voenizdat, 1966.
2. Yu. S. Russian, *Through the War on 'Babies'*, Moscow Voenizdat, 1988.
3. I.I. Azarov, *Odessa Besieged*, Moscow Voenizdat, 1962.
4. *Submarines in Attack: Collection of Stories*, Moscow DOSAAF, 1985.

Chapter 8
1. G.K. Zhukov, *Memoirs and Reflections*, Moscow Olma-Press, 2002.
2. D.I. Ortenberg, *June–October 1941*, Moscow Soviet Writer, 1984.
3. V.N. Novikov, *On the Eve and in Days of Great Ordeal*, Moscow Politizdat, 1988.
4. A. Yakovlev, *1941, Documents*, Volume 2, *Moscow Democracy*, 1998.
5. A. Osokin, *Great Secret of Great Patriotic: An answer to an Enigma*, Moscow Vremiay, 2010.
6. A. Drabkin, *I Fought on T-34*, V. 2, Moscow Yauza, 2007.
7. Petr Delyatitsky, interview with Artem Drabkin, http://www.iremember.ru/.
8. Grigory Sinyavsky, interview with Artem Drabkin, http://www.iremember.ru/.
9. Mariana Milyutina, interview with Artem Drabkin, http://www.iremember.ru/.
10. L. Osipova, *Unknown Siege*, Spb, Neva, Moscow Olma-Press, 2002.
11. Vera Pirozhkova, *Lost Generation*, St Petersburg, Neva, 1998.
12. Yulia Drounina, *Selected*, Moscow, Fisction, 1981.
13. N. Shpanov, *The First Blow: A Novel of Future War*, Moscow, 1939.
14. Lev Poushkarev, interview with Artem Drabkin, http://www.iremember.ru/.
15. Ibid.
16. Nikolai Doupak, interview with Artem Drabkin, http://www.iremember.ru/.
17. Tamara Ivanova, interview with Artem Drabkin, http://www.iremember.ru/.
18. N. Ovsyannikov, *Farewell, Boys*, Moscow Yauza, 2007.
19. Sophia Fatkoulina, interview with Artem Drabkin, http://www.iremember.ru/.
20. A. Drabkin, *I Fought on T-34*, V. 2, Moscow Yauza, 2007.
21. Igor Samoroukov, interview with Artem Drabkin, http://www.iremember.ru/.

22. A. Drabkin, *I Fought on Po-2*, Moscow Yauza, 2008.
23. Valentin Rychkov, interview with Artem Drabkin,
    http://www.iremember.ru/.

Conclusion
  1. Adolf Hitler, *Hitler's Secret Conversations 1941—1944*, trans. N.
     Cameron and R.H. Stevens, with an introduction by Hugh Trevor-
     Roper, New York, 1953, p. 59.
  2. *Izvestia*, 4 July 1941.
  3. Konstantin Simonov, 'Wait for Me', poem dedicated to Valentina Serova,
     published in 1941.